THE Heart OF HOUSTON

Lessons in Servant Leadership

FOREWORD BY STEPHEN L. KLINEBERG, PH.D.

COLLECTED AND WITH AN INTRODUCTION BY
LAURENCE J. PAYNE

bright sky press
HOUSTON, TEXAS

bright sky press
HOUSTON, TEXAS

2365 Rice Blvd., Suite 202
Houston, Texas 77005

ISBN: 978-1-936474-79-0

10   9   8   7   6   5   4   3   2   1

Library of Congress Cataloging-in-Publication Data on file with publisher.

Portraits of servant leaders by Katherine Tramonte, Horseshoe Studio, horseshoestudio.com

Bright Sky Press would like to thank Brittany Fox and Julie McKinney
for their generous assistance with *The Heart of Houston*.

Editorial Direction, Lucy Herring Chambers
Editor, Eva J. Freeburn
Creative Direction, Ellen Peeples Cregan
Design, Marla Y. Garcia

Printed in Canada through Friesens

This book is dedicated to my father, Melvin Payne, 1922-1982, a spiritual giant whose motto was, "if God says the same." A native son of St. Landry Parish, Louisiana, he was a dedicated parishioner of St. Therese's Roman Catholic Church, a member of the Knights of St. Claver and a motivated servant leader of "salt of the earth men" at Levingston Ship Building Company in Orange, Texas.

And to the late Archbishop James P. Lyke, Archbishop of the Archdiocese of Atlanta, Georgia, OFM, my mentor and spiritual director of many years in servant leadership. Archbishop Lyke was the first African American Archbishop of the Roman Catholic Church in America. He installed me as the first lay vicar in the U.S. Roman Catholic Church as Vicar of Urban Affairs for the Diocese of Belleville, IL., which included East St. Louis, named "The poorest city in America" in 1980. Every day of my life there was truly an opportunity to serve.

I am very grateful to the many people and the relationships forged throughout my life that have made this book possible. To those who provided support, a listening ear, a patient heart, and the fuel to ignite this passion. But most importantly, to my friends and colleagues who've become my family. For agreeing to document this journey, I am forever indebted to you all.

To the individuals I have known, served and labored with, in this great vineyard known as HoUSton—thank you!

Servant Leadership is the foundation upon which community is built and flourishes. Servant leadership in the United States is exemplified in the heart of Houstonians, and lies at the heart of Houston and its communities. When we help others reach their full potential, we not only come closer to reaching our own, but we build lasting connections that tether us heart to heart.

FOREWORD

This is a really wonderful collection of essays from an impressive group of Houstonians, all contributing to an assessment of the meaning and importance of "servant leadership" in our time. These are some of the heroes—there are many more, of course, who could readily have been included in this collection—who are working selflessly behind the scenes to strengthen our community and to help build its collective future.

Leadership of this sort may be needed more right now than ever before in Houston's history. The region faces a daunting array of challenges and opportunities in its efforts to build a truly successful society in the new world of the 21st century. Houston is in the midst of remarkable change, reflecting more clearly and sharply than most other cities the basic trends that are refashioning the economic, political and social landscape across all of urban America. How this region navigates these transitions will be important not just for the Houston future, but for the American future as well.

The restructured economy and the growing inequalities. The resource-based industrial-era economy, for which this city was so favorably positioned, has now receded into history, taking with it the traditional "blue collar path" to financial security. In its place, an increasingly unequal, high technology, knowledge-based and fully global economic system has been taking shape. Gone forever are the days when a high school graduate with few technical skills could go to work as a roustabout in the oil fields, or on an assembly line at Hughes Tool Company or Cameron Iron Works, and expect to be able to earn a middle-class wage.

The transformations brought about by globalization ("the rise of the rest"), along with advances in science and high-tech automation, have polarized the available jobs, creating growing inequalities that are predicated above all else on access to quality education. In a survey conducted by the Kinder Institute in 2012, 76 percent of Harris County residents agreed with the statement that, "for a person to be successful in today's world, it is necessary to get an education beyond high school." Only 22 percent believed instead that "there are many ways to succeed with no more than a high school diploma."

It is particularly disturbing therefore to learn from a recent study funded by Houston Endowment Inc. that fully three-fourths of all Texas students, who were followed for 11 years after beginning 8th grade in 1996 to 1998, had not earned a certificate or a degree of any sort beyond the high school diploma, even six years after their expected high school graduation date. If we are unable to change those outcomes and to provide Houston's underserved young people with the credentials they will need to succeed in the new economy, it is hard to envision a prosperous future for the region.

As these essays show, servant leaders are helping to expand access to health care (May, Mullins, Jones) and to quality pre-school programs (Houston). They are working to derail the "cradle to prison pipeline" (Gilmore), to build schools that reach out to and nurture newly arriving immigrants and their children (Moreno) and to bring college students and poor children together to turn public housing into centers of joyful learning and personal growth (Jackson). Servant leaders have also created Houston's amazing charter schools—YES, KIPP, Harmony—that are models for educational reform across the country.

Much more will be needed along these lines if we are to ensure that Houston's young people acquire the skills they will need to thrive in a knowledge-based economy. May the essays in these pages serve as inspirations for us all!

The new importance of quality of place. From now on, a city's prosperity will have less to do with its control over natural resources and more to do with human resources. This region's prospects will increasingly depend on its ability to nurture, attract and retain the "knowledge workers" whose creativity and skills are the primary generators of wealth in the new economy.

To compete with other metropolitan areas across the nation, Houston will need to develop into a more aesthetically and environmentally appealing urban destination. The region must continue to make significant improvements in its "livable centers," its green spaces and recreational areas, its air and water quality, its mobility and transit systems, its venues for sports and culture, the quality and visibility of the arts in all of their manifestations.

Here too servant leaders are contributing importantly, by repairing neighborhood parks (Bell) and improving the quality of the air we breathe (Frels). It was this kind of leadership that helped convince the voters in the 2012 election to support a $100-million bond initiative to transform Houston's ten major bayous—waterways that had basically been paved over and neglected through most of the last century—into an interconnected system of linear green spaces and recreational trails, creating an iconic park system that will help to reinvent this city for the 21st century.

The demographic revolution. After the oil bust in 1982, Houston's Anglo population stopped increasing and then declined. Virtually all the growth of this burgeoning region over the past 31 years has been due to the influx of Latinos, Asians and African-Americans. This traditionally biracial, Anglo-male-dominated Southern city has suddenly become the single most ethnically and culturally diverse large metropolitan region in the nation.

With its young, multi-cultural and multi-lingual workforce, Houston's diversity will surely be a tremendous asset for this major port city as it builds the connections to the global marketplace. Yet if most area residents continue to live and work in largely segregated enclaves, reinforced by widening economic and educational disparities, the increasing diversity will instead diminish the region's competitiveness, fueling the rapid growth of an "underclass" of Houston's citizens who leave school without the skills they need to find a decent job and setting the stage for serious social conflict.

If this city is to flourish in the years ahead, it will need to grow into a much more equitable, inclusive and united multiethnic society, one in which equality of opportunity is truly made available to all area residents and all of its communities are encouraged to participate as full partners in shaping the Houston future. This community will need to build many more and sturdier bridges across its racial, ethnic, faith/religious and socioeconomic divides, and such bridges will not be built on their own. The essays in these pages give eloquent testimony (Hellums, Marshall, Kollaer) to the personal and collective importance of the many innovative programs—Leadership Houston, American Leadership Forum, Center for Houston's Future—that have been reaching out to the region's diverse leaders to strengthen the relationships that will empower area residents across Houston's varied communities to join in the collective effort to build a truly successful multiethnic future.

As this collection of essays makes clear, Houston's greatest resource is the quality of the people who live here, the many quiet heroes who care deeply about this community, and who exemplify in the very way they live their lives the commitment to helping others reach their full potential. Only servant leadership of this sort, practiced on an ever wider scale, will enable this community to respond effectively to the remarkable challenges of our times. These essays give powerful witness to the ways Houstonians can work together to secure that better future.

Stephen L. Klineberg, Ph.D.

INTRODUCTION

For each of us, there are times that spotlight and magnify the most important things in life. Sometimes it can be a personal accomplishment, like the birth of a child, or it can be the passing of a loved one. For me, it was a stroke.

In June 2006, I had just finished delivering the closing plenary session address for the Father William J. Young Social Justice Institute at the University of St. Thomas when I was walking to the parking garage and fell over. Luckily, my friend, Deacon Joe Ribbio of Catholic Charities, found me and called 911. And I was rushed to Memorial Hermann Emergency Room by the great EMS team from Fire Station 16. Leading up to this moment, I had experienced some dizziness, some numbness in my left arm, and some blurred vision, but I thought nothing of it. I thought I hadn't eaten enough or that I was tired. This, however, all proved untrue. I was surprised when medical staff informed me that I had suffered a stroke. I had had no previous history of high blood pressure, nor did I have high cholesterol. How could *I* have had a stroke?

The cause, they told me, was stress. Two months later, in August 2006, I suffered another stroke.

During my recovery I came to two very important realizations. I needed to be proactive about my health, and I was here to encourage servant leadership. I needed to share the value of both practices with others.

We need five things on a daily basis to maintain good health: proper nutrition, proper physical activity, attention to mental health, spiritual growth and laughter. Don't just be proactive about the warning signs, I'm always telling people, be proactive about your health. We must take care of ourselves in order to be healthy enough to serve others—a truth that is closely related to my second realization. During my time in the hospital and in recovery, I was surrounded by people who were willing to give me a helping hand. With the care and love of innumerable people, I recovered. It took eighteen months, but I reached full mobility again.

Throughout this experience, I encountered many people who embody the term servant leader—someone who leads by serving others, someone who puts others first. One nurse stands out in particular. After I had been rushed to the hospital's emergency room, it was there that she first reached out and held my forearm with her hand. There was so much love, warmth, power and care in that one squeeze! Her eyes were warm at that moment; I was her sole worry, her sole charge. She effortlessly put another human being before herself. This nurse so comforted me with the warmth in her touch that later, when I went to work for Memorial Hermann as a consultant, I sought out the nurses that worked in the ER that day, and in a blind test had them line up to squeeze my arm. The other nurses were not surprised when I identified her in the line up. Our lives are measured by the four 'Ts', and we often forget about the *fourth* one: time, talent, treasure, and the most important—touch. Servant leaders are servant leaders in every way; they reach out to encourage and inspire others everyday building relationships through touch.

That nurse's action was so important because she reached out to me, one human being to another. She exemplified *true servant leadership*— manifesting the understanding that life is not all about the self. It is about the *other*—someone different from myself; someone that does not look like me—the other person who we should be serving. *Servant Leadership* is the philosophy and practice of leadership, as defined by Robert K. Greenleaf, founder of the Center for Applied Ethics. It is a management style, a technique that focuses on people, work and community spirit, with a deep understanding of identity, vision and environment. In the most basic sense, a servant leader is one who leads by serving his or her community. In Greenleaf's own words:

> The servant-leader is servant first... It begins with the natural feeling that one wants to serve, to serve first. The conscious choice brings one to aspire to lead. That person is sharply different from one who is leader first, perhaps because of the need to assuage an unusual power drive or to acquire material possessions... The leader-first and the servant-first are two extreme types. Between them are shadings and blends that are a part of the infinite variety of human nature.

Joseph Jaworski, the founder of American Leadership Forum, had this to say about Robert Greenleaf:

> The moment I saw the words Servant as Leader, they had an enormous impact on me. The very notion of servant leadership was absolutely stunning to me, and I couldn't put it out of my mind. It was as if someone had suddenly cleansed my lens of perception, enabling me to understand what I had been struggling with for so long; at the same time, it was as if a memory of long ago had been reawakened.

I created the following, entitled *Servant Leadership Framework,* in order to help others visualize the basic principles of the philosophy.

Begin on the top left of the circle with *Vision.* The first step in being a servant leader is to know yourself and what you believe, aligning what you do with what you think. By doing this, you grow as a person, inspiring and developing servant leadership in others. This requires you to be proactive—that is, to do important things instead of just talking about them. Being proactive allows you to lead by example. People respect consistency of thought and action. Checking your actions, ensuring they align with what you believe is the right thing to do, entrusts that you take personal responsibility—*Accountability,* the top right of the circle. This step is critical in the *Servant Leadership Framework,* as holding yourself accountable for your actions and beliefs builds the habits that help you grow as a leader. As a servant leader, you are not only accountable to yourself, but also to your community. You exemplify the word *us*—the idea that the world is not about *you*, or *me*, but is instead about the togetherness of *us*. You understand that to be the best leader in your sector, you must first be the best servant in your sector. Once you've held yourself accountable, you are ready to move down to **Implementation,** to foster that same behavior in your peers. This is your follow-through. This means you not only attempt to do the right thing, but you also do the right thing in the right way. It means caring about and nurturing others; it means putting the needs of others before those of your own in a way that builds relationships, teams and communities. The leader who not only insists on alignment of mind, body and spirit, but also does the right thing in the best way possible, is a ***Servant Leader.***

THE SERVANT LEADERSHIP FRAMEWORK

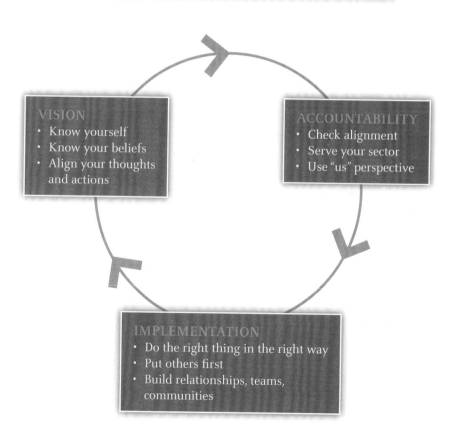

VISION
- Know yourself
- Know your beliefs
- Align your thoughts and actions

ACCOUNTABILITY
- Check alignment
- Serve your sector
- Use "us" perspective

IMPLEMENTATION
- Do the right thing in the right way
- Put others first
- Build relationships, teams, communities

Servant leadership defines human beings in a certain way. It points to relationships rather than individuals. It is a leadership based on service first, setting aside stories of fear and competition and replacing them with stories of possibilities and potential. It calls us, as a community, to look at who we are: Are we ready to dialogue and listen, to grow, to learn, to share, to work, to serve each other? Servant leaders should be willing every day to question and challenge people as to why they are not being servants, and why we as a community, are not being a servant leadership community.

A servant leader wants to make a difference for other human beings, listen to perspectives that may differ from their own, empathize and heal people. Servant leaders are aware of the world around them. They look at the big picture and are future-oriented for the greater good of all human beings who make up society. They want everyone to grow in their personal, professional and public lives, and they have a strong sense of community and of community building.

If we can grow the practice of servant leadership, a strong community will follow. The servant leadership community will make our tomorrow and our collective future possible. The highest goal of a servant leadership community is to enable others to succeed, to make sure every human being is reaching their full potential. For truly, in the end, as Benjamin Mays says, "For not failure but low aim is sin." So aim high, aim high!

We can see this concept of servant leadership in every sector: business, religion, education, healthcare and many more. In education, a servant leader is someone who exhibits and expresses unconditional love for all students, regardless of race, religion, gender or ability. It is someone who nurtures each human being under his care, who does everything in his power to help those he is educating. In healthcare, a servant leader is someone who approaches those she cares for with warmth, care and concern, exemplifying in every breath, every movement, that she cares, that she nurtures, that she heals. This philosophy can exist in every industry because it is applicable everywhere.

My fifteen-year journey as a host of the weekly call-in radio program *Interchange*, 90.1FM KPFT and the weekly community affairs television show *Dialogue Houston*, HCC-TV, CH19, led me to deeply examine the recurring theme of servant leadership. Many of the guests I've interviewed have given powerful examples of what it means to be a servant leader through their life of service to our community. Both shows gave me the opportunity to interview inspiring examples of passion, of empathy, of compassion and of care. I began to see what the common thread was: all those I interviewed were outwardly centered. They didn't seek rewards or recognition; they did their work truly from the heart.

No matter their race, creed, color or church, servant leaders gravitate toward each other; they know each other. There is a huge circle of servant leaders, who cover all walks of life. Servant leaders find each other because they share more than the same language; they share the same concerns about consistency between thought and action—they are not talkers, but doers. They have all lived and exemplified the classic example of adulthood, seizing the opportunity for creativity and initiative instead of complaining about what cannot be done. A servant leadership community is a doer community.

Servant leadership is not just a theory, but something practiced by many throughout Houston. It is time for them to step into the spotlight. They are powerful contributors to Houston. Though financial success tends to get the loudest praise, it's time for those who serve the community to share their voice, visions and passions, and be celebrated. This book is a way for the servant leaders of Houston to share their stories, to show how servant leadership has played out in their careers and to receive recognition. We often don't recognize their contribution, or the impact they make—because they're not seeking recognition. When we look closely, we realize that despite their focus on the needs of others, people work hard for them. In this way, these leaders create success.

The Heart of Houston presents servant leaders in our community in their own words, as they share their own vision of servant leadership in the scope of their experiences and pursuits. When I invited them to share their thoughts, I purposefully left the prompt open-ended. Though there is a definition of servant leadership, it manifests as individually and uniquely as each person practicing it. Each leader has taken a different approach to explaining servant leadership. Seen collectively, these stories clearly illustrate that one person, one touch, even one voice, can truly make a difference—in the recovery of a stroke victim, in the healing of a community and in building a better life overall.

Servant leadership asks us to go above and beyond the call of duty for everyone our lives touch. Is it possible to live this way? As you read the following essays and concepts, you'll see that not only is it possible, it's happening all over Houston. And you, too, can be a servant leader, whatever your industry or sector.

TABLE OF CONTENTS

Though the concept of servant leadership has its roots in business and religion, its branches are far-reaching. In the essays that follow, you can identify tactics and traits of servant leadership and align your management techniques accordingly. Some of these essays are tactical; some share the path of how successes were achieved; all are inspirational. They by no means have to be read in any order, or as a whole. They are stand-alone glimpses of inspiration, dedication, conviction and insight. They provide a window to the ways some of Houston's greatest leaders were able to create success for others, for their teams, for their communities and ultimately for all of us—through serving.

Following the essays you'll find information about servant leadership to help you put these practices to work in your own organization.

Inspiration
FROM
Servant Leaders
IN
HoUSTON
BUSINESS

Rogelio (Roger) Marroquin is Director of Client Operations for the Global Document Outsourcing Division of Xerox Corporation; he is also a member of the National Hispanic Professional Organization and its Leadership Council.

YOU HAVE TWO EARS, ONE MOUTH

When I was asked to share my thoughts about servant leadership, I felt it would be important to first share how I have developed those thoughts over the years. I arrived in this country when I was very young. My parents, both with only grade school education, valued hard work and truly believed that working hard was the only way to make a living. As I fast forward through my junior high and high school years, what I experienced was that by working with and helping others, my work became easier, both at my part-time restaurant job and in school projects.

After high school and many, many interviews later, I was fortunate to earn an entry-level job with a Fortune 500 corporation. With thirty-two years behind me and continued work with the same corporation, I have been blessed with extensive formal education and executive development programs, as well as first-hand experience in many different leadership roles and positions, both at work and in my community, that have shaped my servant leadership behavior and thoughts. Ironically, it was the expanding of my early experience of working with and helping others that have made life and work easier and more rewarding.

So what are my thoughts about servant leadership? In a nutshell, servant leadership is about caring for others and their values as you do for your own, while you accomplish desired goals.

How does caring for others translate into servant leadership? Caring for others means you must effectively:

- *Listen.* As my grandmother would say, "God gave you two ears and one mouth, therefore you should listen at least twice as much as you speak." But to really listen, one must do more than just hear. You must listen and understand with true empathy to be effective.
- *Set expectations.* In order to help others, two-way communication is critical. Not only is it important they understand what is expected of them, it is necessary for them to understand what they should expect from you.
- *Set accountability.* Theirs *and* yours. Once expectations are shared and understood, setting accountability is required to set boundaries and, in return, to share control with the people you are leading. The better everyone understands how each person is accountable, the better the outcome of the expected results will be.

While effectively listening, setting expectations and accountability are key to caring for others, I have concluded that servant leadership is demonstrated only when personal integrity and a passion for the good of others are ingrained into the DNA of a servant leader.

Jim Kollaer, FAIA, LEED AP, Managing Director at Kollaer Advisors, LLC, provides services to international and corporate real estate clients. A licensed architect, he is the former CEO/President of the Greater Houston Partnership.

HOW DO YOU KNOW WHAT A SERVANT LEADER IS?

"To lead people, walk beside them ... As for the best leaders, the people do not notice their existence... When the best leader's work is done the people say, 'We did it ourselves!'" – **Lao-tzu**

There is a saying in the service professions, "You don't really know how bad an amateur is until you have worked with a professional, and you don't know how much a professional has to learn until you work with a true master." This can be applied to the servant leader question as well. You really don't know what an egotistical leader is all about until you have worked with a true servant leader.

This is the story of one servant leader, Joe Synan. I call him Father Joe. He entered my life through our association with the American Leadership Forum (ALF) in the 1980s. Synan has been involved with ALF since the eighties as an advisor and former national board member. His impact on the ALF leadership program still grows as its dream reaches its 30th year.

Synan is an amazing person, one whom I would certainly offer up as an example of servant leadership in my life. Not only has he learned the philosophy of the servant leader, all ten characteristics outlined by Robert Greenleaf in his early papers, but he has also taught and practiced it for as long as I have had the pleasure of calling him my friend. He is the embodiment of the servant leader and is passionate about it.

Joe is humble, as you would expect of a servant leader. But, if you dig into his background you will find that he has three degrees in nuclear engineering and math, all from Notre Dame and MIT. To balance all that "hard edge" engineering knowledge, he has a masters in Religion from St. Thomas University. For the last twenty-five plus years he has led a company called Leadingwell Associates, a firm dedicated to helping businesses, institutions, organizations and individuals stretch for the future. The firm applies the servant leader philosophy to help their clients achieve their goals. Joe has led a life full of rich experiences, from his years at Gulf Oil and Chevron to ALF and Leadingwell. He brings everything he has learned to everything he does and to everyone he meets. Today, in addition to his consulting work, he is a teacher, an accomplished runner, experienced mountain climber, student and watercolor artist.

There is one sentence in the Leadingwell mission statement that, for me, characterizes Joe and his core philosophy: "Leadingwell Associates is totally focused on the client and how the client can be helped, serving clients with no consciousness of financial arrangements..." and goes on to state, "Leadingwell Associates performs a wide variety of challenging assignments, working for and with friends."

One of the many instances when I have seen his servant leadership demonstrated occurred when I was having a particularly difficult time in my role as CEO of the Greater Houston Partnership. The Greater Houston Partnership is the leading non-profit business organization in the Houston region. It was created from a roll up of the Greater Houston

Chamber of Commerce, the Houston World Trade Association and the Houston Economic Development Council. When I became CEO in 1990, we had a board of 55 CEOs representing the major business organizations and political entities in the region. We had 2,000 businesses as members and an equal number of volunteers to carry out our annual program of work that focused on public policy, economic development and improving the quality of life for the region. We addressed the major sticky issues in the big areas of public policy including education, healthcare, environment, transportation, economic development and world trade.

We were in the middle of some strategic issues and we were stuck. Joe called to say that he was going to come down to the Partnership and work with us for as long as we needed him to help. He said that he saw areas in which he could help make a difference and perhaps smooth out some of the rocky times we were experiencing. I was blown away by that offer and accepted it without hesitation. "Pay is optional," he said. The key for him was to help his friend—me—and to give his time. That is Joe. Together we solved the problem.

On another occasion, Joe decided that he was going to climb to the highest point in each of the 49 states before he got too old to do it. He invited a number of us to join him on any of those treks that included a wilderness adventure. Ultimately, Joe climbed to the highest point in over 40 states. Several of us joined him on mountain hikes and together we have had "peak experiences" on those summits. Those were true learning journeys and transformative times for all of us who went along. Joe organized and led those adventures.

Another time Joe stepped forward to invite those of us who had climbed with him to join him and some newfound friends to have dinner at the "River," an imaginary place where we could break bread together and continue the conversations we started during our climbs.

We became the "River Group," and at monthly dinners we shared each other's lives and our roles in changing the world. Each of us shared Joe's desire to help, and most of that help took place behind the scenes. Synan always made the dinners interesting and informative so that we could help each other to grow in our respective roles in the community. We addressed and solved some pressing issues for Houston and the organizations that we represented. Those dinners were off the record like all the other "learning journeys" Joe led. We discussed successes and failures and made new friendships thanks to Joe. His impact on our lives and our careers has been amazing. We would never have had the richness and depth of experience had Joe not cared for us and taken the lead in making our ideas a reality.

In the title of this essay I asked, "How do you know what a Servant Leader is?" You know when you meet someone like Joe, or dozens of others who are quietly leading and growing their companies or institutions, growing their people, healing communities and stretching us to adopt the ethics and principles that are the core of servant leadership.

Lidya Osadchey is the Founding Executive Director of the Holocaust Museum Houston. In May 2000, she was appointed CEO of ESCAPE Family Resource Center.

RISE UP, GET UP!

I knew it was 6 A.M. A small wall radio, blasting the Red Army Choir's song, incited the Soviet citizens to spring from beds and get on with the day, "Rise up, get up, working people!" We did as ordered even if it was our day off. Growing up in the former Soviet Union inculcated us with the mindset of submission to authority (especially wearing an army uniform), private and public life meshed. A person's destiny was a cleverly charted and prescribed path by the government. One voice counted only if it were in the cacophony of a choir. Orders from self-serving party bureaucrats, not the individual pursuit of happiness; commands, not yearning of the heart; acquiescence, not eagerness—all were precepts lining our Soviet DNA for the benefit of the society at large.

Ironically, this song rang in my ears when, at 20 years old, I decided to emigrate and seek a more fulfilling future than the former U.S.S.R. could offer. The blatant anti-Semitism I experienced along the way finally reached its apogee at the university level. I wanted a chance to live my own life, tapping my strengths and talents, not in the U.S.S.R. I yearned to explore the gifts and blessings of my Jewish heritage and the canons of the free western world, not in the U.S.S.R. Now or never, I told myself, *Rise up, get up, working people!* Time to go! Having borrowed thousands of rubles to pay for the exit visas, the loss of citizenship and the freight of some of our personal belongings, my mother and I finally left the U.S.S.R. After three months of living like *personae non gratae* in Austria and Italy, the Jewish Agency supported us; we crossed the Pacific Ocean and landed in New York. What a sweet memory I have of seeing the Statue of Liberty for the first time. I had goose bumps all the way down the landing strip!

It was October 23, 1977, when my mother and I exited the Houston Intercontinental Airport and ventured outside into unimaginable heat and humidity. If tears and pain accompany birth, then it is only expected that the rebirth would trigger the equivalent emotions. I never forgot that day, and I still celebrate it annually. "Rise up, get up," the shock! We were moved to an apartment on Gasmer Street in the Westbury area. We were given a stipend to cover four months of rent, food and some miscellaneous items. People knocked on our doors and brought food. Neighborhood kids, also immigrants, taught us how to use bank checks. Two families were assigned to help us acculturate in America. They were volunteers (not ordered or commanded) with the Jewish Federation of Houston. We could not forget Susan Ganz, who came with her three tiny children and a stroller filled with bags of food, or Celine Kaplun, who on our fifth day in Houston, rang the doorbell with her mother-in-law and said, " We will be your family here!" And they have.

We were perplexed that strangers volunteered to help us. Later, I found out that our trip from Italy and the entire immigration procedure was completely underwritten by the Jewish community. I was in amazement that people voluntarily parted with their own hard-earned money, organized our arrival, undertook the collection of furniture and household items, scheduled English classes and drove us to doctors' appointments. The intricate and well-coordinated system of adaptation of the former Soviet Jewry into life in America was an eye-opening experience.

I was hungry for knowledge about my Jewish roots. I wanted to be a part of the community that takes in strangers and makes them feel at home.

I WANTED TO BE LIKE THOSE PEOPLE…WELCOMING, GIVING, RELIABLE AND PROUD!

Those thoughts have guided me throughout the passing of years. I met people who inspired me, too many to acknowledge in a deserving way. School, work, family, friends and community volunteer commitments occupied every waking minute of my life. Still, I longed for a perfect project that would allow me to apply all my past life experiences and education. The project found me when I was offered the job of Founding Executive Director for the Holocaust Museum Houston.

It may be hard to imagine that the Holocaust Museum Houston, which has achieved national and international fame, faced a time when the doors closed shut at the mere mention of building it. Asking for support, financially and in-kind, invited a score of excuses and explanations as to why it was such a badly timed idea. We heard it all, from references about the recession to the fact that a National Holocaust Museum was already being built in Washington, D.C.

I will never forget my first and only encounter with a Houston businessman who did not ask any of those questions when I came to see him in his office early on in the project. As a matter of fact, Mr. Irving Kaplan expressed his gratitude to me for coming to him for help. He told me how thrilled he was at the prospect of building a Holocaust Museum in Houston. He thought it would be a wonderful educational institution to keep the memory of our Jewish people alive through the stories of the survivors and liberators from Houston. I really needed to hear those encouraging words, as the frustration was slowly building in my system. Mr. Kaplan, who had recently been challenged by health and business issues, pointed to his lumber yard and said, "This is all I own right now. You can have it. Build the Holocaust Museum!" He rose to bid me goodbye, handing me a list of his friends' names to call for support. I was feeling recharged. Before I could spring from my seat and make it to the door, Mr. Kaplan was already dialing the phone to give a heads up about my impending calls to his contacts.

A CARING WORD AND THOUGHTFUL GESTURE CAN CHANGE YOUR WHOLE PERSPECTIVE ON THE TASK AT HAND.

True leaders have that effect on people without trying. I had just met one, and I knew I wanted to be like Mr. Kaplan. A short time after this meeting, we increased the visibility of our educational programs in Houston. We were ready to announce to the world our inspired mission: to build a Houston institution, for all Houstonians, of all religions, races and origins. To do that successfully, the Board of Directors planned to launch an all-out effort to broaden the base of support, from the Jewish community to the community at large. We knew that it could be accomplished with the right leaders at the helm. A list of names to lead this campaign was short. The name "Ben Love" was synonymous with power, lucid eloquence and sartorial grace. In the late 80s, Houston was still struggling with the aftershocks of the deep recession. Not just Houston, but all of Texas. The only bank that made money for its shareholders in those bleak economic times was Texas Commerce Bank, with Ben Love as its CEO. Mr. Love's name opened doors and loosened deep pockets. He was a recognized leader in our community, and beyond; and he raised millions of dollars for a wide range of causes and non-profit organizations.

I met Mr. Love for the first time through an introduction by Mr. Sanford Alexander, CEO of Weingarten Realty. A very successful businessman and an esteemed civic leader, Mr. Alexander agreed to be the founding chairman of the Circle of Tolerance (COT). He welcomed me in his office with a warm smile and assured me of the great value of our project for the city. COT, a corporate arm of the Holocaust Museum Houston, was charged with raising funds in Houston's business community. We asked him to invite Mr. Love to be his co-chairman. We knew that, while a student at the University of Texas, Mr. Love had enlisted to serve in the Navy during the Second World War. He was assigned to the 8th Air Force flying B-18 bombers as a navigator. He had completed his 25 missions and was about to volunteer for another round when the war ended.

What we did not know then was that Mr. Love personally witnessed the results of Nazi atrocities perpetrated against the Jewish people. He was ordered to fly to Mauthausen Concentration Camp to bring back the surviving prisoners of war. Mauthausen was classified as a "category three camp." For its prisoners, mainly Hungarian Jews and Russian soldiers, it meant "Rückkehr unerwünscht" (return not desired) and "Vernichtung durch Arbeit" (extermination through work). The lasting painful memory of that mission and his absolute commitment to fair treatment of people based on merit and not on race, gender or religion, influenced his answer. He said, "Yes," and promptly launched into his duties.

Honestly, I was both excited and nervous to work with Mr. Love. I had heard stories about his demanding style and meticulous attention to detail. He was also a history buff and his memory was legendary. What if I failed to make a good impression on him? Thankfully, we developed a genuine respect and affection for each other. That led me, many years later, to have full access to Mr. Love, his work and personal files, while I was working on his biography in graduate school.

What I vividly remember from working with both Mr. Alexander and Mr. Love shaped my own interpersonal and leadership style, and prepared me well for the ensuing professional challenges. Both men showed enthusiasm and expressed support for the nascent project. That took courage, as we were an unknown at that point. They listened deeply and asked a lot of questions about their roles as co-chairs. Without delay they got on the phones themselves (this was before email and texts) and made appointments to solicit support. They did not delegate their duties to assistants. I was often stunned at how available they made themselves for our project. After all, those two men were sought after by both the business and the philanthropic communities. They were modest in accepting gratitude and, instead, lavished praise on those who signed up to work with us.

Real leaders listen and learn from people around them. When they agree to take on a commitment or a job, they see it through by putting forth an immense personal effort. They do not seek recognition or glory, and make room for others to shine.

Writing about servant leadership prompted me to look back at 34 years in America and examine them carefully, asking myself if I lived up to my potential. Hopefully, not yet. I learned a great deal from many people who encouraged me and supported me, and from those whom I failed. I learned **gratitude** by listening to the stories of Holocaust survivors who marched forward with the joy of life, in spite of unspeakable tragedy and cruelty inflicted upon them and their families. I learned **courage** from people who stood up for what they believed, even in the face of social isolation. I learned **acceptance** from my dear friends who conveyed their unconditional love over the years, providing a safety net when I thought I was in a free fall. And I learned **patience** by trusting staff and volunteers to peak in their own time while I provided encouragement and fortitude.

If there is a better way to feel one's own pulse beating in sync with the needs and wants of the community than adding to its vitality, I have not found it. Having seen my own children "Rise up, get up" and weave their care and talents within the communities where they live, I am only that much more assured in the legacy of my teachers.

Kelly Frels is a Senior Partner of Bracewell & Giuliani LLP. He is an emeritus member of the Greater Houston Partnership Board and is the Chair of the Texas Environmental Research Consortium.

CLEAN AIR AND QUALITY OF LIFE – BUSINESS LEADS

In the fall of 1998, the Chair of the Greater Houston Partnership Board told his Executive Committee that Houston had a clean air problem that had to be addressed. Ansel Condray, President of Exxon USA, charged the business leaders of the Greater Houston Partnership (GHP) with cleaning the air.

Houston had the dubious reputation of having some of the worst air in the country in the late 1990s, almost as bad as Los Angeles. High concentrations of ozone presented a health hazard, and not meeting the ozone standards of the federal Clean Air Act was certainly a public relations problem. The Houston area's failure to meet the legal requirements could affect its eligibility to receive federal transportation funding—an intolerable possibility for a fast-developing city that depended on highways for travel.

Houston's local governments, including the city of Houston and the Houston-Galveston Area Council of Governments, had not addressed solving the air pollution problem, and the governmental leaders apparently had no immediate plans to do so. Thus, the business community took the lead in reducing the Houston region's ozone levels.

Contemporaneously with the need to reduce the levels of ozone in the Houston region came the recognition that the quality of life in Houston needed enhancement. Houstonians were not pleased with how the city looked, with its many billboards and lack of public landscaping. Residents also expressed concern about the availability of parks, hike-and-bike trails and other amenities. Business leaders pointed out that Houston's quality-of-life reputation, coupled with dirty air, was adversely affecting their companies' ability to recruit employees to Houston. Banker Charles McMahan, along with a leadership class of the Center for Houston's Future: The Region's Think Tank and others, urged the business community to improve Houston's quality-of-life.

Faced with these serious needs, and a lack of leadership from the city of Houston and other responsible governmental entities, the business community acted through the Greater Houston Partnership and crafted a corrective plan. The action focused on reducing the ozone levels and enhancing the quality-of-life, while maintaining Houston's vibrant growth economy—a very ambitious goal.

The Greater Houston Partnership leaders created the Business Coalition for Clean Air (BCCA), a 501(c)(3) organization that was chaired and ably led by GHP board member and former Secretary of Energy, Charles Duncan. The BCCA raised several million dollars from GHP members to fund a community effort to improve air quality that was centered on engaging businesses, working with governmental officials, developing ozone control strategies and getting helpful legislation passed. A major focus was educating the public on what causes ozone and what actions each person or business could take to help control its contribution to ozone. (Ozone is formed when chemicals classified as volatile organic compounds combine with nitrogen oxides. Hot days with little or no wind are ideal for ozone formation.) The development of the campaign, "Clean Air, It's Everybody's Business," featured informational publications and television spots, some of which included school children, concluding with "Clean Air, It's Everybody's Business." John Nau of Silver Eagle Distributing led the development of the community education campaign. His company led by example, importing "green" diesel from other states to operate its fleet when green diesel was not available locally.

The business community developed plans, made speeches, conducted meetings and educated its members and the public about the challenge to clean the region's air while maintaining a vibrant economy. Many lawmakers were engaged in the passage of the Texas Emissions Reduction Program (TERP), which provided essential funding for air quality scientific research. The legislative effort, led by GHP vice-president Ann Culver, was developed by the GHP leadership and sponsored in the Senate by Senator James "Buster" Brown, and in the House by Representative Warren Chisum.

The Environmental Protection Agency (EPA) recognized the GHP community education and involvement program by asking the GHP and the BCCA to co-host a national workshop with the EPA on community involvement in Washington. A number of cities facing clean air problems have sought guidance from the GHP on how to set up effective organizations and plans.

The GHP then created the Texas Environmental Research Consortium (TERC), which has worked closely with oilman George Mitchell's brainchild, the Houston Advanced Research Center, to use TERP funds to advance air quality science. TERC research, undertaken with the predecessor of the Texas Commission on Environmental Quality (TCEQ), led to the identification of the role of highly reactive organic compounds coming from refineries and petrochemical plants, generally during "upsets" and startups of industrial plant units in the formation of ozone. The results of these studies and other research conducted by TERC guided companies in effectively and economically decreasing emissions. The results were central in the regulators' development of the Houston-Galveston-Brazoria region's State Implementation Plan (SIP) for the one-hour ozone standard. The Dallas-Fort Worth region also benefited from other TERC research in the preparation of its region's SIP.

The GHP, headed by Vice-President George Beatty, led in the creation of the Texas Clean Air Working Group (TCAWG), a loosely knit group with statewide clean air stakeholders. TCAWG meets in Austin with the assistance of the Texas Conference of Urban Counties. This networking group, with representatives from governmental entities, businesses, environmental interest groups, councils of governments, TERC, the EPA Regional Office and the TCEQ, plus other interested parties, meets to discuss clean air strategies. The TCAWG meetings also aid in the development of understanding and trust among the groups that have wide and sometimes competing interests. The GHP provides a businessperson as co-chair of the group with the other co-chair coming from a governmental entity in the Dallas-Fort Worth region.

Developments, such as the infrared camera technology used to identify leaks of volatile organic compounds, higher national standards for automobiles and truck engines and other technology-related developments, have been significant in the accomplishment of lowering levels of ozone. The GHP encouraged volunteer efforts on the community level, such as businesses converting fleets to natural gas or using clean diesel or engine retrofits. Governmental entities, including the city of Houston and Harris County; the Port of Houston; Continental (now United) and Southwest Airlines; the railroads and other businesses joined the effort and took actions to decrease emissions. Federally mandated cleaner fuel standards and engine manufacturing requirements also played significant roles in ozone reduction.

While the GHP leaders were successfully helping reduce the ozone levels in the region, the organization also took a lead on improving Houston's quality of life. A GHP Quality of Life Committee was established and facilitated networking among numerous independent quality-of-life-focused organizations.

The Quality of Life Committee addressed tightening Houston's billboard regulations and securing state set-aside funding for the landscaping of freeways and state highways. Graffiti removal and general cleanliness were high on the agenda. Planting and maintaining trees along city streets was a priority undertaken by Trees for Houston and similar groups. The city of Houston, the Houston Independent School District and the reinvestment tax districts began to include landscaping in their building plans.

Tropical Storm Allison brought major flooding to Houston June 6th through 8th in 2001. The flooding caused major damage at the Texas Medical Center in downtown Houston, and throughout the city. The GHP's Houston Area Flood Control Task Force brought the Harris

County Flood Control District and the city of Houston together with others to evaluate the flooding problem and to plot solutions. The city is responsible for getting the water to the bayous and major waterways, and the Harris County Flood Control District is responsible for moving the water to the bays. Through the efforts of many, federal funds were secured, and over the years some of the major bottlenecks for water flow have been corrected. The hike-and-bike trails system and the development of parkland along the bayous are in large part derivative of the discussions after Allison.

The Quality of Life Coalition emerged as the umbrella organization to address quality-of-life issues. Through the efforts of many, Houston today looks very different from the Houston of the past, with the most positive aspect being that quality-of-life considerations are now a part of virtually everyone's planning and implementation process.

In 2010, the Houston region met the eight-hour ozone standard. This marked a milestone for the effort to clean Houston's air. The quality of Houston's life is noticeably improved, and the city is receiving national notice for what it is today. The business community in Houston played a huge role in these achievements—as servant leaders whose leadership was joined by many others. Much remains to be done because the federal ozone level has been lowered. Meeting the tougher standard will require a significant effort from business, governmental entities and all in our community. We can enjoy our success, but we must keep our eye on providing for the future. We have done it, and we can continue.

Gordon Quan is co-chairman of FosterQuan, LLP. In his long history as a community activist, he has served on City Council, as Mayor pro-tem, and as a member of the Board of Directors of many area organizations, such as the Coalition for the Homeless, the South Texas College of Law and Neighborhood Centers, Inc.

WALKING THE TALK

In his biography, automobile maker Soichiro Honda shared that early on in his company's development he crawled on the floor of a squat toilet to retrieve the dentures of a valued client, cleaned the dentures, and even tried them on to ensure their cleanliness before returning them to the client. Honda believed that he could not ask someone to do something that he himself was not willing to do.

Being a servant leader means walking the talk. We cannot ask others to do what we ourselves would not do. And we ourselves must do what others are not willing to do. That is servant leadership.

The name each person likes to hear most is his own. We seek the praise of others. We yearn to be popular. These are natural human feelings. Doing a job but seeing others get the credit, or faking a popular but unprincipled stand on a controversial issue—these rub us the wrong way. Still, I believe that God sees all that happens, and He knows our hearts and minds. Who are we a *servant* to? Our egos, society or a higher being?

I am inspired by the words of St. Francis of Assisi who said, *"Preach the gospel at all times. Use words when necessary."*

Inspiration
FROM
Servant Leaders
IN
HOUSTON
EDUCATION

Marie Moreno is Principal of Las Americas Newcomer (4th-8th grade) *School, a member of American Leadership Forum, Association of Hispanic School Administrators, Houston Association of School Administrators and the Gulfton Youth Development Program.*

CLOSET OF HOPE

The most valuable possession anyone can attain in the world today continues to be an education. Gone are the days when having one skill or trade was all that was needed to get ahead in life. Disappeared is the era when agricultural careers could provide a quality standard of life. The technological world unfolding around today's students require these young adults to have the same set of knowledge and skills once taught to students expected to fill the blue collar workforce in addition to a more defined formal education and testing standard. In order to secure any

21st century job, where computers and modern medicine are not only the *new* way of life but are also the *only* way of life, all students are held to the national *No Child Left Behind* standards.

No longer the city dominated by Anglo-Americans, Houston blossomed into a city full of diversity where people from all over the world come to live the elusive and alluring "American Dream." More and more immigrants and refugees are now enrolling in our public schools, forcing educators to change the way we teach and run schools to make a better tomorrow for everyone.

Being a servant leader stems from my career as a principal of a small middle school in Southwest Houston. We serve students primarily from the Gulfton Community, which is heavily populated. The 3.197 square miles just south of Southwest Freeway 59, bordered by Rice Avenue, Bissonnet Street and Hillcroft Avenue, is home to 46,287 people. That's about 14,477 individuals per square mile. It's the densest community in Houston! It is here that many agencies, such as Catholic Charities, Interfaith Ministries, International YMCA and Alliance, find homes for the refugee families they sponsor. Las Americas Newcomer School is an English Intensive school for these and other newly arrived students.

Serving these students has not been an easy task. Just eight years ago, Las Americas Newcomer School was predominately serving only Hispanic newcomer children. Students were usually exposed to concepts and content that were no different from those at the school down the street. Thus, children were not acquiring the English language fast enough to perform on the state's high-stakes tests. Something had to change. It was my mission to travel the country and learn from others who were serving other such unique populations.

We serve students in grades four through eight who have been in the country for less than two years. We currently serve students from thirty-two countries, and they speak twenty-two languages. It is by far the most diverse school in the Houston Independent School District. Our mission is to acculturate students to this *new* world by teaching them survival skills, to assimilate them to the American school system and to teach the English language so they can be better served when they feed into comprehensive high schools.

A team of teachers and I visited successful programs in Fairfax, VA, St. Paul, MN, and Brooklyn, NY. We studied classrooms, reviewed the educators' ideas and tried to obtain the knowledge needed to create a successful program that could address our unique population. During that year, we noticed an influx of students coming from Iraq, Sudan, Somalia, Congo and Ethiopia. The population seems to be forever shifting, depending on what country had a war break out, or which country is in the midst of a revolution. There was no turning back. We knew that the methodologies we taught our children in the past were no longer going to work with these children of tomorrow. We *had* to change.

We have successfully completed the fourth year of our transformation. Here at Las Americas Newcomer School, we focus on the whole child. We cannot just focus on the academic side of a child's life and expect them to be successful in this *new* world, this *new* life and this overall *new* environment. It requires us to be ultra-sensitive to the students' surroundings and extra careful to help them overcome the barriers and obstacles set in their paths so they can continue their journey to *a new beginning.*

Running this unique school takes a leader with a vision and a true commitment to ensuring all students' well-being; someone who not only looks at education, but the environment around the school to ensure that success. I remember one morning when Sara came to school. I was outside supervising students as they walked in to the school as I did each morning. She was limping. Anyone could see she was in a lot of pain. I leaned over and tried to understand what was wrong without the luxury of a shared language. Sara was a new student who spoke not one word of English yet. Using gestures and simple English I said, "You, why limping [as I limped a few steps to show the action she was doing]?" She then pointed at her shoes. As I removed her old tennis shoes, I realized that her shoes were two sizes too small. She had blisters along the edge of all of her toes. She had no other shoes to wear and she did not want to miss school. We quickly sought out medical attention for the blisters, and purchased some sandals from a nearby store. This small act prompted the beginning of our *Closet of Hope.*

The *Closet of Hope*, which has recently been adopted by a non-profit organization, is a boutique-style room where students can "shop" for clothes from donations made by teachers, staff, other students and the community. We were able to fill it with clothing in all sizes for both males and females. When students enroll at our school, we first ask if they have the basic school essentials like paper and pencils. If not, we provide them with a book bag full of basic school supplies and necessities. Our next question is if students have clothing to wear to school.

Many families arrived in Houston with only the clothes they were wearing. Acquiring school uniforms, or any clothes that fit, is always a challenge. At Las Americas, families are able to "shop" for clothes along with other family members at no charge. Many families take this opportunity to obtain essential clothing for job interviews or everyday clothing. We have been fortunate to have many people donate gently used or new clothes to our closet. When the kids are in need of a jacket, jeans or just another shirt, it's nice to hear, "Miss, can I go to the closet? My shirt is getting too small and I need to get more."

Not only is clothing a necessity, but health services are crucial when it comes to families that for the most part have never seen a doctor for a basic physical. Hermann-Memorial Healthcare Systems has a site-based clinic on campus. Students are eligible to obtain medical services for free. Here, students get yearly physicals, immunizations and medical services when they become ill or get an infection. The clinic dispenses medication, at no charge. We also have a dental van that comes quarterly to see students for any dental needs, free of charge. One year we had a group of Sudanese students smiling from ear to ear, "showing off" their new braces.

Once we have taken care of the student and family's health and essential needs, working with them to learn English is that much easier. They have the drive to learn because they already know that we care enough to help them, not only in school, but out of school as well. It takes a very special teacher to work with such an amazing group of kids. Each student has a story to tell about the challenges they faced in getting to America, and that makes them more determined to learn.

Teachers at my school have to go through extensive training in language acquisition. We focus on listening, speaking, reading and writing in every subject, in every class, every day. Every student is tested and placed in a group based on their language proficiency level. We begin by meeting the student at his academic ability level, and then our job is to get him ready for a mainstream setting. In any given classroom, we may have up to eight languages spoken. It is a sight to see and hear. Seeing Afghanis working in collaboration with Iraqis and hearing Somalis working with Nepalese and many other nationalities truly reflects the world of tomorrow. We have to teach all our students, realizing that we are no longer a nation of one or two nationalities, but a nation of many nationalities coming together to build a better future for America's tomorrow.

Our data now shows our success. We have monitored our students for the past four years to see growth patterns. Many of our students show between one and two years of language acquisition in only one year. The state requirement is to show the minimal growth of one year. With many of our students enrolling at our school at the pre-literate stage, not knowing their first language proficiently, this is already a huge accomplishment. Other students do so well that the state no longer allows the state refugee or language exemption to be utilized on the state's exam because they out-perform students born in the U.S.A. who have attended school since pre-kindergarten. Schools from all over the country now come to tour our school to see how we are dealing with Houston's influx of refugees from all over the world and how we are achieving our success.

None of this could be possible without the help of many individuals and organizations. I may have the vision, but collectively as a group this mission has become a reality. Partnership for the Advancement and Immersion of Refugees (PAIR) works in collaboration with our school to provide after-school programs and enrichment activities to expose students to events that schools may not be able to afford with today's budget constraints. Baylor University's *Cloud Search* is a mentoring program that allows a 2:1 ratio between students and mentors and interns studying counseling. The lead teacher, Raquel Sosa-Gonzalez, a visionary and a pioneer in newcomer strategies, is a crucial piece of our school's success. She has the passion, heart, patience and vision to seek the success for all the students who attend Las Americas Newcomers School.

As educators, we have an obligation to teach our students for the future, but we must also take a hard look at ourselves to see if what we are teaching is reaching the students of today's classroom. The world is changing at a swift pace; educators must recognize this and must advocate innovative changes for our students. Since high stakes testing is not going away, it is imperative we allow schools and school districts to work with all unique populations. It takes years to acquire English prior to being measurable by tests of academic knowledge. Once a student learns the English language at a level sufficient to be successful on the state tests, he or she will then be more successful in reaching mastery levels in all subject areas.

As students graduate from high school, many return to their roots—where their journey began. They are grateful for the foundation Las Americas provided each of them that has ensured their success in obtaining a high school diploma. Many have become productive citizens in society with dreams to attend a post-secondary school to further their education and impact within society. Educators preach that we can no longer accept a high school diploma as the ultimate accomplishment, but we should see it as a stepping-stone to what lies ahead in their future. It brings a sense of satisfaction to me, every day, that we actually change lives—lives that may have been derailed if the pathway was not created and promoted to ensure every student's success.

Put yourself in their shoes. Imagine leaving a place you have called home for many years, living in environments and conditions that most of us could never imagine. Then imagine attending a school that has high expectations for you to perform at your very best, to learn a language you never thought you could grasp, all in a short amount of time. The journey our students take is simply unbelievable. We, as educators and as human beings, encourage this journey every single day. Every day at least one new student enrolls in Las Americas and begins his new journey.

We are proud of the work we have accomplished; however, we realize that in order to continue teaching and educating, we can *never* stop learning. New challenges arise every day, and we must have the vision to see and overcome those barriers—one student at a time, one step at a time. That is servant leadership in action.

W. Robert Houston, *Ed.D., Professor Emeritus at the University of Houston since 2012, is the director of the Partnership for Quality Education and the author of more than 40 books and hundreds of journal articles and research papers.*

The Servant Leader Influences the Most Vulnerable of Society—Its Youngest Children

SERVANT LEADERS COME WITH DIFFERENT STYLES

One day, we attended a memorial service in Lubbock, Texas, for Harold Harriger, my only brother-in-law who had passed away the previous week. Harold had been an attorney, a leader in his church and in civic affairs for half a century. As people told about his life and accomplishments, at least two individuals quoted one of his favorite sayings: "It's the right thing to do! Let's do it." He used it often in making recommendations about controversial issues, and he lived by this tenant. He was known for settling disputes, bringing people together, making progress by collaboration and for not making the expedient decision but one based on "doing the right thing" and "doing it in the right way."

As I examined the Servant Leadership Framework in the front of this book, I thought about Larry Payne's life and leadership, and I thought about Harold. I began to realize that the important changes in the ways we live and educate future generations are made by people who are not *self-serving* but are committed to *other-serving*. This volume is dedicated to *servant leaders,* and their *unflinching dedication to a better life for all.*

There are many men and women who are examples of servant leadership in our community—in schools, churches, non-profit organizations, businesses and universities where I have been privileged to work—and their goals, strategies and intentions could be described as illustrations of this concept. But the individuals from one program stand out as paramount.

From its inception ten years ago, I have served as the external evaluator for the *United Way Bright Beginnings* program, and thus have objectively observed the activities of the persons involved in the program—the leadership in United Way of Greater Houston and ExxonMobil, child care specialists and consultants, and particularly the directors and teachers in *United Way Bright Beginnings* centers. I have marveled at their impact on children and their contributions to early education of young children. These small non-profit child development centers serve economically disadvantaged communities, are committed to "making a difference" in the children and families they serve and, from the program's beginning, have epitomized the tenets of servant leadership.

IT TAKES A COMMUNITY TO MAKE A DIFFERENCE

During the past thirty years, Houston has experienced major changes in the ethnicity, age and spoken language of its people, often being described as the most diverse ethnic city in America. As the 21st century unfolded, community leadership, including the United Way of Greater Houston and ExxonMobil, considered the issues and potential strategies to bring about changes in the most persistent problem areas. They sought strategies that promised long-term change, and committed themselves to making a difference. Their deliberations and subsequent actions were those of servant leaders.

In 2001, the United Way of Greater Houston and ExxonMobil committed themselves to embark on a long-range mission to make a difference in Houston by committing themselves to improving the quality of early childhood education for disadvantaged children. The lack of quality early childhood education was a persistent problem tied to the future, not only of the children themselves, but also of Houston. The decision by these two organizations was vital and far-reaching.

Children do not enter kindergarten or first grade as "blank slates," yet for many children, particularly underprivileged children, school begins at this age. At age five or six, some children are ready to read, calculate and interact with other children, while others struggle to complete the simplest activities. Yet, these early differences are "powerful predictors of later school achievement, economic productivity, and a lifetime of physical and mental health, " according to a 2006 study by Knudsen, Heckman, Cameron & Shonkoff. Emerging research on the brain supports the need for rich experiences and emotional support during the first five years of life, while "persistent negative experiences are potentially toxic for the developing brain, " Grindal, Hinton & Shonkoff asserted in 2012. "Abundant evidence indicates that emotional development is inextricably intertwined with cognitive abilities and physical well-being," found Hinton, Miyamoto, & Della-Chiesa in 2008. "Chronic or traumatic experiences such as homelessness, unremitting poverty, abuse, or neglect can have severe and long-lasting consequences on children's brain development," according to the United Nations in 2006. Early childhood caregivers "play a critical role in nurturing healthy development in the face of traumatic or persistent stress," said Grindal, Hinton, & Shonkoff. The need and the mission were clear.

And so, the *United Way Bright Beginnings* program was born, funded by generous support from ExxonMobil, and powered by community leadership in early childhood education. The program evolved over the past decade as it studied effective programs for young children, focused on extensive professional development of teachers and directors, provided age-appropriate resources to centers, and tested the effectiveness of each innovation.

In 2012, eighteen childcare centers were part of *United Way Bright Beginnings.* The program has resulted in extensive changes in the education of pre-school children, primarily from disadvantaged homes. The classroom environments are different, the teachers different, and the organization of the centers and the quality of resources are relevant to improving children's lives.

Making these major changes requires a committed core of devoted professionals—servant leaders—including the eighteen center directors and over 200 teachers who engage in extensive professional development activities, implement the most current and viable instructional procedures and content, and experiment and test new ideas. Annual observations of every classroom demonstrate the major improvements in their work with children, changing environments of classrooms and playgrounds, and the more effective use of age-appropriate materials and equipment. Our observations, surveys, interviews and analyses of test results have confirmed that the program has improved each year and currently is one of the best in America. These teachers and directors are, indeed, servant leaders who are committed to making a difference in the lives of children.

The program owes its vitality and evolving quality to the leadership of individuals who have dedicated themselves to the development of the program, not as a job, but as their commitment to the Houston community and its future citizens. They have individually exhibited the characteristics of servant leaders. These servant leaders include Amy Corron, Katherine von Haefen, and Linda O'Black of United Way; Marcela Clark of Collaborative for Children; and the directors of *United Way Bright Beginnings* child development centers. The program's success is based on the commitment of these leaders, as well as the teachers in the centers, the Advisory Committee and the myriad of consultants who provide focused professional development. These are the servant leaders in our community and the ones to be applauded for their major contribution to young children's development.

TAKING ACTION ON INTENTIONS AND OPPORTUNITIES

About 35 years ago, serving as a consultant and advisor, I had the privilege of designing the curriculum for the Free University of Iran. On what turned out to be my last trip to Iran, the University's Vice-Chancellor took me on a trip around the country to experience the program we had been working on for several years. We stopped at Persepolis, the ancient capital of Persia, magnificent even in ruins today. As we stood in the shade of one of the giant pillars, a man came up and told us a fable that I shall never forget, one that I believe describes a major attribute of servant leadership. It is the story of a lion that thought he was a goat. The baby lion had become lost as a cub and raised by a herd of goats. He learned to eat grass, make strange noises, and stay with the other goats for protection. One day, a majestic beast, with a flowing mane, came bounding across the plains toward the herd. The little lion/goat had a primordial feeling of kinship with the huge lion, a feeling he should be with him, join his lifestyle. But instead, he turned and ran away with the herd of goats.

The moral of the fable is this: For one brief moment, the lion had the opportunity to be what he was meant to be, but instead he chose simply to be a member of the herd. For many, the security of the herd keeps them from reaching out, assuming leadership, making a difference in their community, their job or profession. They simply remain part of a group, a willow waving in the breeze, while their potential becomes a passing vision, enjoyed and forgotten. The servant leader steps out, tests the waters of a new venture, does the right thing, and encourages others to do likewise. That is how society develops, becomes stronger, more personal, more influential—not through the work of those who choose the anonymity of the crowd, but through the efforts of those who do the right thing.

Valerie D. Jackson, *Ph.D., is the Executive Director for Solutions for Better Living. She serves as Treatment Director at the Wings of Refuge Family Service Agency, Adjunct Professor for Houston Community College and Lone Star College and is a clinician at the Wellness Counseling Center Psychology Department.*

iSERVE: SERVICE LEARNING PROGRAM

My first experiences with civic engagement were weekly projects that I participated in as a member of the church youth ministry at age eight. My father was the youth pastor of a small progressive church, and the senior pastor gave him the flexibility to operate the youth ministry in the best way he saw fit. My father was very innovative in structuring the youth program. It consisted of many opportunities for community involvement and leadership activities. We conducted projects such as community clean-ups, assisted with political campaigns, volunteered at senior citizen day programs, organized holiday events for underserved communities, maintained a food pantry for the church and facilitated drives for causes (i.e. blankets for the homeless, school supplies and Christmas gifts for children from disadvantage families, etc.). My father allowed the youth to plan the initiatives. He made it our responsibility that these civic activities be executed, so we understood that this was our project and its success or failure was hinged upon our efforts. We were taught lasting leadership skills while serving our community. At the time I did not view this as servant leadership. I was just excited to be involved with project planning and spending time with friends in the youth ministry. I did not know this experience was shaping me for the work I am so passionate about today.

These early experiences influenced my choices of professional and personal involvement in servant leadership. I have participated and organized many community projects since childhood. One of the first companies that I opened was a nonprofit organization that provided resources (i.e. clothing, beds, food vouchers) to families in need. The idea for this organization derived from my work as a community-based social worker. I would refer my clients to agencies and organizations that allegedly had certain resources. Unfortunately, when my clients would try to access the needed resource they often were told the resource had been exhausted for the month. In order to have an inventory to meet their needs, I decided to start collecting donated items that my clients might request. From that first venture I have expanded to assisting visionaries of civic projects with implementing their own ideas. Over the past twelve years, I have assisted over 100 nonprofit organizations or philanthropic projects to get started.

Currently, I am an executive director of a community development organization, as well as a college professor. Often, when I have introduced the concept of servant leadership to my students, they have stared blankly back at me, puzzled. They, like many adults, conceptualize the term *servant* as a lowly person, not one they wish to strive to be. After some discussion, several students believed there were those servants, like those who work for the Queen of England, whose positions were well respected. However, for the most part, most admitted their perception of the role of a servant leaned more toward the peasant role-playing that one might witness at a Renaissance Festival or Medieval Times depiction. That is to say they believed the life of a servant to be inconsequential and powerless. Further, those who choose to serve most likely have little ambition and probably no interest in gaining power or influence.

As we delved further into the theory and underlying principles of the servant leadership model, I explained to them that much of what they supposed about the dynamics of power and influence is to the contrary. I am never surprised when they remain skeptical. Even when I have offered various examples, such as Martin Luther King, Mother Theresa, Nelson Mandela, President Bill Clinton and Rosa Parks, figures they undoubtedly viewed as influential, they remain unconvinced.

We are living in era of unparalleled wealth and advanced technological innovation. What human beings have achieved over the last two decades has created endless possibilities for our future. Some believe that in the next twenty years we may possibly bring world hunger to an end, eliminate chronic disease and send anyone interested in space travel to the moon. But with that said, we also live in what many view as the most turbulent time in the history of the world. Every day we are witness to the images of economic turmoil and violent social upheaval. It occurs in every part of the world, even here in the large cities and the main streets of the U.S. The case could be made that much of what has been accomplished in the fields of finance and science now fuel a never ending, greed-driven struggle for wealth and power that causes these crises.

It has become apparent that most people, no matter where they live in this world, believe there is a critical lack of leadership at every level of their government—education, religious institutions and financial sectors. Where is the cognizant and ethical leadership we so desperately need at this point in time? Although there are some voices that offer our communities hope in the form of new ideas, there seems to be no end to the number of political demagogues, social critics and made-for-television talking heads willing to shout over each other anytime we're willing to tune in—one more outraged and determined than the next, vying to gain our support for their social, political, religious and economic platforms that many times only serve to fan the flames of the anger, distrust and resentment flickering between us during these difficult times.

My students are part of a generation that research says is less inclined than its parents and grandparents to become involved in social issues. I have combed over countless academic studies and sat in numerous meetings where we have explored sources of the leadership vacuum and come up with an exhaustive list, so I know the reasons for their lack of involvement is not clear cut and cannot be generalized. Though it probably seems somewhat sanctimonious and out of touch, I would be less than honest if I didn't admit that my students, and the other young people I meet, seem to lack commitment to anything that isn't attached to acquiring wealth or extending the fifteen minutes of fame they seek through Facebook, Twitter or YouTube. Their lives are being tossed about and pummeled almost daily by constant generational, cultural and technological waves that bring about the transformation of ideas, beliefs and, many times, their perceptions of what it means to be powerful, honorable, courageous and moral. What have we done to the next generation's servant leadership skills?

The community development projects that I've organized as the executive director of *Solutions for Better Living* (an affiliate of the Dreyfus Health Foundation) are primarily focused in Houston's Third Ward. On October 29, 2010, Preston Middleton (GM TSU TV/ Comcast Technology Consultant / Adjunct Professor at Texas Southern University) invited me to a student meeting on the campus of Texas Southern University. Twenty-five students attended the meeting, and they expressed an interest in becoming more civically involved. Texas Southern University is a historically black university that has a long-standing history of promoting the value of community involvement and student activism (i.e. alumnae—Barbara Jordan, Mickey Leland, and the 1960 lunch counter sit-ins). While some of the fraternities, sororities and department-based groups on campus are involved in some kind of community service, most of the students do not participate in volunteer programs. But ten years ago, TSU operated continuing education and health related programs that utilized student volunteers and benefited the public housing facility. Unfortunately, since that time, no organized outreach efforts have been made. This is particularly troubling when TSU, an HBCU with over 11,000 students, sits directly across from the Cuney Homes apartment public housing complex. The housing project is home to well over 2,000 residents, who are predominately African-Americans living below official U.S. poverty lines.

The following meeting on November 19, 2010, served as an opportunity to develop an action plan, known as iServe. During the same meeting, a TSU senior was elected as a student leader. It was determined that the goal of iServe is to improve academic achievement among school-aged children residing in Cuney Homes and the surrounding area by offering mentorship, tutoring and academic enrichment activities. iServe is a community-based service learning program that is organized and operated by TSU students with the assistance of *Solutions for Better Living* staff.

On March 26, 2011, iServe Third Ward was launched on the grounds of Cuney Homes. Over 35 school-aged children were enrolled in the program. Every week more than 20 Texas Southern University students are at Cuney Homes assisting over 50 children with homework, conducting educational activities (i.e. math competitions, spelling bees and reading exercises), playing sports, performing dance routines, engaging in poetry/writing activities and providing individual mentoring. We have observed the children's increased interest in school, education and learning activities, as well as improvement in their behavior. The children view the TSU students as their role models and are excited each day about engaging in activities with them. The TSU students reported feeling a connection with the children. The experience has heightened their awareness of the importance of being actively involved in the community. The program challenges these young adults to think about their values and the community issues they care about. It also encourages the critical thinking skills needed to develop and implement strategies to address problems they've identified as important.

The program is in the second year of operation. Students from other college and universities (University of Houston, Lone Star College, Rice University and the University of St. Thomas) began volunteering with iServe, and the program has retained some of the original students from TSU. They assist with leading the initiative and training new student volunteers. The students have developed curriculums and added components to the program. In February 2012, a second site was started on the grounds of Kelly Village Housing Development in Fifth Ward. At this site we conduct academic enrichment activities and health education that includes nutrition classes, organized sports and a fitness program. Over 35 children and ten college students participate in the program weekly.

iServe has been an exciting experience for me personally. I have observed the growth of the program over the past two years. It has been ideal to promote civic engagement and encourage servant leadership with college students. It appears that once the college students become involved they understand the needs and become passionate about delivering service to better the community. For these students the gateway to getting involved is the need to obtain extra credit for a class or to meet the volunteer requirements for a major. Nevertheless, the student is exposed to serving the community. iServe not only positions them to serve their community but also gives them the opportunity to share their ideas and implement projects in order to improve the overall program. iServe is a college-student designed and operated program. The students enter the program with the idea that they are volunteering, but in actuality they are leading an education reform movement.

Servant leadership to me is a selfless act. It is placing others' needs above your own desires, comforts or wants. It's taking action even if you don't feel like it because you know it's the right thing to do. Money does not change the world. People do. Change can only happen if people mobilize and take action against those things that plague our society and hinder us from having the best world. Some people do not realize the power that they possess when they apply the right action to a situation. Doing the right thing can change the dynamics of an entire community. It just requires taking the first step—*action.* I've met many people who are conducting phenomenal works in their community. From their point of view, they are executing something they are passionate about. They do not realize that they are exhibiting characteristics of an effective servant leader. It is important that we support and assist the work of our servant/community leaders. During the process of assisting someone else with a community initiative, we could connect with our passion. Many things can transpire while serving. It all starts with identifying the need and taking action. That is how change happens and lives are impacted significantly.

Inspiration
FROM
Servant Leaders
IN
HOUSTON
RELIGION

Most Reverend Joseph A. Fiorenza, Archbishop Emeritus *of the Archdiocese of Galveston-Houston, currently serves on the Board of Christus Health Foundation; the William A. Lawson Institute for Peace and Prosperity; the Neighborhood Recovery Community Development Corporation; Catholic Charities Community Development Corporation; Catholic Relief Services Foundation; and the Center for Faith and Culture of the University of St. Thomas.*

LEADERSHIP

There are many definitions of leadership but there is one trait that all leaders possess: vision. Without a clear and certain vision one cannot expect to inspire others to follow "an uncertain trumpet." The ability to articulate the vision in a persuasive manner is also critical to a good leader.

There is an ongoing debate about whether leaders are born with certain traits of leadership or whether these essential traits can be acquired.

I will leave this debate to psychologists and those who are experts in human behavior. Whether born as a leader or not, a leader must be one who is willing to listen to those he or she will lead. Today, people are more willing to follow a leader who does not use authority or position as a means of demanding others to comply with his vision as a desired goal. Rather, people are more likely to follow a leader because a vision has been presented to them persuasively.

Every effective leader is also one who is passionate about a vision and can inspire others not only to accept his vision, but also to give themselves totally to the cause; he or she is able to bring out of them their very best efforts. The leader, of course, must not demand of others what he or she is not willing to do. Leadership by example is a powerful incentive to enlist the cooperation of others.

While summoning others to a common vision, a leader is not fearful of engaging those who may be more knowledgeable or more experienced than he is. In such cases, the leader's challenge is to engender enthusiasm for his vision. This can only be achieved if the leader is comfortable with talented people and is not threatened by ideas that may conflict with his vision of reality.

Abraham Lincoln is a good example of this. He had the capacity to bring his opponents together to serve in his cabinet, and he encouraged their talents to preserve the union. They served as a team of rivals but worked together to end the Civil War and slavery. While being a team of rivals, Lincoln was able to make them feel like a team in pursuit of a common vision.

A good leader is always willing to listen to his or her co-workers and is willing to reconsider some strategies in pursuit of the vision. The willingness to reconsider earlier ideas or plans is a sign of a humble leader. It is also a sign of integrity.

The ideal of a servant leader is found in Jesus, the founder of Christianity. Of himself he said: "I did not come to be served but to serve." His whole life was a life of service to those most in need. He captured the essence of Christian service when he instructed a young follower to demonstrate love for God by a love for neighbor, as one would love oneself. Later he gave an example of servant leadership when he washed the feet of his apostles and said he had given them a model to follow.

Since the time of Jesus there have been, among many, two outstanding followers of his message of service to others. Fifteen hundred years ago, St. Benedict was an outstanding leader. He established monasteries throughout Western Europe that were the beginning of a monastic system which brought education to illiterate people, and served as bulwark against the dark ages. Benedict wrote a rule of life for his monks, which is still followed today among Benedictines around the world. The very first word of the Rule of Benedict is, "Listen." Benedict wanted his followers to listen to God and to one another. He believed we could learn not only from God but also from one another. A leader who disregards what his co-workers are saying will soon find that they are also not listening to him. Benedict was aware that God's Spirit often speaks through others.

The other example from the Christian era is St. Frances of Assisi. In the Middle Ages, Frances started a revolution of people who were willing to follow him by a radical living of the Gospel. An outstanding rule of St. Frances was the ability to enter into the experience of others as the culminating expression of mission in Christian life. To love one another, Frances taught that his followers should always consider the place or condition of another, and try to put themselves in the shoes of the other. A true leader will always have some experience of the condition of others. It is this experience that helps form his vision and fills him with a passion to transform the vision to reality.

Again we can look to Lincoln as a good example of putting oneself in the place of others, to experience what they were feeling and to understand their situation. His great empathy with the plight of slaves motivated him to make the abolition of slavery as central to his presidency.

I like the distinction of Peter Ducher—doing things right or doing the right thing: One speaks of being efficient and the other of being a leader. They are not opposed, and often a good leader is also an efficient leader. But it is more important to be a leader with integrity than an efficient leader without it. Without integrity a leader will soon lose the ability to attract others to follow him.

General Colin Powell described a leader as, "Someone unafraid to take charge. Someone people respond to and are willing to follow." I agree. A leader must be decisive. One who is hesitant to make a decision, especially when decisions must be made, will not be able to inspire others to follow his lead. A hesitant leader betrays the idea of leadership.

No one definition of leadership can capture all the dimensions of a good leader. I have mentioned some, which I think are important and which I have observed. Whoever is called to a leadership position should not only consider the honor and responsibility of being a leader, but also should give serious consideration to the traits of leadership that I have identified.

Reverend William "Bill" Lawson is founder and Pastor Emeritus of Wheeler Avenue Baptist Church in Houston. He was honored with the creation of the William A. Lawson Institute for Peace and Prosperity (WALIPP), a non-profit advocacy agency serving the underserved in Houston's Third Ward and surrounding areas.

MY PERSONAL PHILOSOPHY OF SERVANTHOOD

This paper modifies the term "servant leader" to the more accurate term by which I describe myself—"servant." I consider myself a follower rather than a leader, because I attempt to obey the orders of One greater than I. My life consists of an effort to follow His commands rather than my own drives. I fail often; but here are the orders He has given to me to follow, and which I try even though I do not always succeed.

Thou shalt love the Lord thy God with all thy heart, and with all thy soul, and with all thy mind. This is the first and great commandment. And the second is like unto it, Thou shalt love thy neighbor as thyself. On these two commandments hang all the law and the prophets. – Matthew 22:37-39

So my philosophy of life is simple: follow the orders (and the example) of the Boss.

I love, honor, revere and attempt to obey God. And because Jesus challenges me that if I feed those who hunger, give drink to those who thirst, take in the stranger, clothe the naked, visit the sick, come to the incarcerated, I have done it unto Him.

So if you see me attempting to follow these orders (even though I often fall short), you will understand that I am not a "servant leader," but somebody who is trying to do what my Boss has commanded me to do.

I will not seek political office. I will not attempt to accumulate capital. I will not seek prominence or power. But I will try to be sensitive to those with neither capital nor prominence nor power; to those who have no voice; and to those who are suppressed by the system. Preacher? Yes, because the powerless need to know somebody will confront the powerful on his or her behalf. "Civil rights leader?" No, because my activities are not determined by an organization or a movement, but by a Person.

What do I believe? I believe God has taught us how to live, and what to do with whatever gifts He has given us. I appeal to all who read these lines to pray for me that I might follow those teachings better tomorrow than I have today.

The Very Reverend Joe Reynolds *served as the Dean of Christ Church Cathedral from 2000 until 2012, and is currently serving on the Board of Directors and Finance/Audit Committee of St. Luke's Episcopal Health Systems; the Board of the Cathedral House Episcopal School; and Cathedral Health and Outreach Ministries.*

A WAY OF LIFE

When I was sixteen, my father didn't know very much. I was born in 1946, he in 1920; the twenty-five-year difference could just as well have been a hundred. World War II was a chasm that separated us in ways both small and profound. We lived in the same house and yet in different worlds.

I know now that my father was a part of what Tom Brokaw dubbed the "Greatest Generation." He had grown up a child of the depression in rural South Carolina, and like most Americans at the time, his life was largely regulated by the seasons and rhythms of agriculture. The so-called "good" war had turned everything upside down, never to be the same again. I think he was always a bit bewildered by how things had turned out.

After the war ended my family joined millions of other citizens who were not returning to the farms but settling in the cities and the suburbs around them. For more than twenty years my parents lived ten or twelve miles outside of Atlanta, Georgia, and my father was never comfortable. He was like a man in a suit two sizes too small, never really at home in his own skin. When he was at home he seemed to be on the constant prowl looking for something to do. He missed the freedom of space that he had found on the farm. He always had as extensive a vegetable garden as possible, even to the point of planting a turnip patch in the front yard where there was better sunlight.

I, on the other hand, grew up a suburbanite. I couldn't have cared less about the garden, and I was easily frightened by creepy-crawly things. My sister and I both preferred margarine to the strong taste of real butter, and buttermilk was an abomination. World War II was ancient history by the time I was old enough to have any awareness of it. I had no notion of the sacrifices made by the generation ahead of me. It never crossed my mind that in some sense they did it for my sake.

My father and I lived by different values; different things were important to us. I was concerned about the latest styles and fads, like Bass Wejuns and madras shirts with a Gant label. If the sexual revolution had not fully arrived by 1962, it was surely beginning to make itself felt. Vietnam was still on the horizon, but the clouds of unrest were starting to bank up. Television was ubiquitous, and with it came all manner of covetousness. We saw into the lives of the rich and famous, and we wanted more. My father didn't have the vocabulary—or the self-awareness—to say it in so many words, but he thought most of what was important to me silly and shallow. Such observations just weren't of his time. His counsel was not something I sought, and his advice, though infrequent, was always quaint and finally irrelevant, anyway. He went his way, and I went mine.

By the time I was twenty-five, my father had grown a lot wiser. I listened to him with a little more attention. I realized that he loved me as best he could. Such expressions were not comfortable or natural for him, so he said it in ways and words that I didn't always understand. The things he lived by—what today we would call "core values"—were simple. He believed in honesty and hard work and doing what you said you would do. When I was twenty-five, that made sense to me.

But there is one thing of which I am absolutely certain: the most important thing in the world is love. Of that I become more certain with each passing year. It was what my father tried to teach me in his own way to the extent that I was willing to learn it. It is love that gives meaning and purpose to life. Love will not make us wealthy, though it will bring us riches beyond our wildest imagining. It will not protect us from hurt or loss, though it will equip us to deal with all the ups and downs that life has to offer. It will not make us strong enough to direct the lives of others, though it will fill us with a different kind of power that comes from sacrifice. If there is to be any kind of final measurement of the lives we lead, the standard will not be how much we accomplished, but rather how much we loved. Love really is the most important thing in the world.

It may have been in something he wrote or perhaps in some lecture he delivered, but M. Scott Peck once said, "Love is the desire for what is really best for another person." It may not be what the other wants or what the other believes is best or needed. It may not be what the other thinks will bring happiness. The question of love is what truly is in the others best interest.

It is the fundamental question for servant leadership. Servant leadership is nothing more and nothing less than the practice of love in the places where we work and live. It is to live in the pursuit of what is good for the other. The action of servant leadership is striving to be the agency that brings the "best thing" to reality.

Servant leadership is not placing the needs of others ahead of your own needs. More often than not, needs don't separate so easily into "yours" and "others'." Wants have a way of becoming needs. Remember, in case of an emergency on an airplane it is important to first put your own oxygen mask on before helping others, even your own child.

Of course, what is best for the other is often not so obvious. It is remarkable how often our own opinions get in the way of seeing the truth. Scott Peck also said "love has to be balanced with humility." "Humility," he said, "is giving serious consideration to the possibility that I may be wrong." Love without humility quickly deteriorates into tyranny even if it is benevolent tyranny. Love without humility becomes manipulation.

The essential discipline of servant leadership is discernment. Faith traditions call it prayer or meditation. The theological expression of the question is: "What does God want for the other, the beloved?" But servant leadership is not limited to the believers of any particular creed. Discernment is a way of living with an open mind and an open heart. It isn't an exercise that gets completed, or a question that gets answered.

We will never know with certainty the answers to important questions, but that is not really the point. The point is asking the questions. We begin with the humility of knowing that we do not know. The question, when taken seriously, moves us dramatically forward in the relationship. The question opens the possibility of new understanding. That is what makes it servant leadership.

Leadership is not limited to those we think of as being in charge or in positions of authority, such as generals, bosses or politicians. We exercise leadership hundreds of times every day in ways that are no less important because they lack dramatic and public magnitude. Each of us has power in our lives. We have choices to make in how we live in a myriad of relationships. Leadership is exercised in the choices we make and the ways in which we make them. We can seek to dominate or to enable. We can strive to control or to love. We have the ability to hide behind the masks of protection or to risk the vulnerability of honesty. Servant leadership is not a principle or a methodology; it is a way of life, and we exact this leadership by learning from those in our lives who love us enough to leave us with questions rather than the answers, but always with love.

My father died when he was a young man of sixty-eight, and I was forty-three. I sometimes wonder how much wiser he would have grown had he lived until I was older. All of which is a roundabout way of saying I don't know as much as I once did. I have fewer answers and more questions. I am okay with that, for I find that as I get older I become more comfortable with questions and more suspicious of answers, especially easy answers to hard questions. I have become aware that the cliché is really true in spite of being a cliché. Life really is a mystery to be embraced and not a riddle to be solved.

Reverend Vernus Swisher is Pastor of Galilee Community Baptist Church; CEO of Career and Recovery Resources, Inc., a non-profit United Way agency; and the current Chair of The Public Safety Advisory Committee for the City of Houston.

FEAR NOT
Overcoming Fear as a Servant Leader

"For God hath not given us the spirit of fear; but of power, and of love, and of a sound mind." – 2 Timothy 1:7

In Exodus 13, the Israelites, after having been enslaved for more than 200 years, are being pursued by the Egyptians. Moses speaks to these decedents of Abraham who have found themselves in the wilderness, lost, hungry and afraid. They are being chased by an enemy who has exhibited great power over their lives. These children of Israel had come to Egypt as members of one family at the invitation of their young-est brother Joseph who, through the providence of God, was placed in charge of Egypt. Though his brothers had sold Joseph into slavery, only the Pharaoh, who had promoted him, was more powerful than he.

God allowed these children of Israel to be fruitful and increase abun-dantly, and the land of Egypt was filled with them. Joseph then died (Exodus 1:6-7). Now there arose up a new King over Egypt, who did not know Joseph. And he said to his people, "Behold, the people of the sons of Israel are more and mightier than we. Come, let us deal wisely with them or else they will multiply and in the event of war, they will also join themselves to those who hate us, and fight against us and depart from the land" (Exodus 1:8-10). Therefore, the new King feared the chil-dren of Israel.

After great afflictions the children of Israel found themselves in the wilderness, led by Moses to the Red Sea. The Egyptian army, with its 600 great powerful chosen chariots, was upon the children of Israel. Most certainly, the situation appears bleak and humanly impossible to escape. But God directs Moses to tell these unarmed and unprepared to fight in-dividuals, to "Fear not, stand still and see the salvation of the Lord which he will show to you today; for the Egyptians whom ye have seen today, ye shall see them again no more forever" (Exodus 14:13). Facing great odds, Moses was being directed by God to lead by exhibiting great trust and faith in Him. I too have personally experienced and witnessed God's great deliverance in many impossible situations.

"Fear not" is a rallying point or catalyst for action related to servant leadership—"*to lead by exhibiting great faith and trust in God*" is the dif-ference between being helpless in a situation or exhibiting great confi-dence to succeed with God's guidance. This is one of the foundational traits you need to possess as a servant leader. The ability to lead by letting go of the fear that can immobilize one from productive action. In my graduate thesis, *A Study of Fear and Addiction,* I discussed the power of fear, but the power of God is greater. "For God hath not given us the spirit of fear, but of power, and of love and a sound mind" (2 Timothy 1:7).

I know strong faith and trust in God has been the hallmark of my professional and ministry career. I have not needed nor depended on an external source for validation. My validation has always been that I know God loves me. When facing overwhelming odds, I have remem-bered the message of the Hebrew Children at the Red Sea.

Servant leadership is about detaching from feelings of fear that impedes excellent performance and success. Your performance when motivated by service to God by serving others can be invigorating. I could be considered a workaholic, but it is through a sense of urgency, understanding and duty that much work is needed to be done. Jesus said, "The harvest truly is plenteous, but the laborers are few. Pray ye, therefore, for the Lord of the harvest, that he will send forth laborers into his harvest" (Matthew 9:37-38). I subscribe to scripture "...To whom much is given, much is required..." (Luke 12:48). Servant leadership will mold itself according to characteristics, traits and parameters of the servant leader, who is being led by the Holy Spirit. Setting high standards and goals are fine if those factors are based on serving God by serving others. My fears—was I pleasing God in my service? Was I doing enough and did the quality of my performance please the Lord? My feeling of not being good enough was not related to a feeling of inferiority but rather was related to the feeling that I must achieve the absolute best to be worthy in God's sight. This led to work behavior in my life that could be considered obsessive, or even addictive in a positive manner.

Fear, the distressing emotion of impending danger was very real to me when I participated in a team mountain climbing excursion as an American Leadership Forum Senior Fellow. The objective of the climb was to help develop teamwork, an awareness of our capabilities and limitations in a challenging environment. People can be fearful, and fear could result in obsessive behaviors in many lives. The key to releasing that fear is to replace it with faith and trust, in God through servant leadership.

Martin Luther discovered this verse in Habakkuk 2:4, "...but the just shall live by faith."

The writings of Martin Luther have significant relevance to what and how fear can affect our behavior. Compulsive or obsessive behavior can result directly from fear. Luther's life could be a case study of how fear played such an important role in his actions and decisions. This fact is relevant to all people with obsessive and compulsive behaviors. They come to grips with their fear when relinquishing to a *Higher Power*—that higher power helps them take control of fear and replace it with faith through their servant leadership.

I have never used drugs nor do I drink alcohol or smoke, but I have a strong work ethic that provides me with an understanding of the frustration of obsessed perfectionism. People in Alcoholics Anonymous know about releasing fears and being accountable, accepting responsibility one step at a time. Overcoming fear is about "the principle of knowledge and acceptance," and working the twelve steps. The steps in overcoming fear and addiction start with acknowledging the need of God's grace. This fosters growth and development and allows you to remain a testament to those around you: You are leading by example, and will thus overcome. This facet of servant leadership at work in the realm of personal and spiritual success can then be transcended into the professional realm.

C. FitzSimmons Allison, author of *Fear, Love, and Worship*, noted that Adam and Eve hid themselves because they were afraid and the fear came from the knowledge that they had been dishonest. According to Mr. Allison, we too hide ourselves...bury our talents and clothe our fears with the fig leaves of fantasy and self-justification. This fear can also lead to obsessive and addictive behavior when we fail to face reality, by using drugs or alcohol, work, eating habits and other behavioral disorders to escape from what is reality. Ever since that time in the Garden, man has looked outside himself for a scapegoat or an excuse. According to Allison, an insurance adjuster once estimated that 90% of people involved in automobile accidents see themselves as blameless. The reason we distort our real situation and clothe it in excuses and illusions is that we are afraid of the reality.

Gary Wendt, of GE Capital, claimed he worked 80 or 90 hours a week at General Electric, one of America's largest corporations. His boss, Jack Welch, was a known demon for maximizing shareholder's wealth, according to Holman W. Jenkins, Jr., in *The Wall Street Journal*, Wednesday, December 10, 1997. He set grueling targets for performance and did not suffer those who failed to meet them. The culture of the organization is based on very high performance and fear of not meeting expected results. Jenkins noted that Wendt testified he was not happy in his job or marriage: "When everybody lives so obsessed by numbers, perhaps a divorce...becomes easier to fathom." Many executives, through fear of not being able to maintain expectations, put themselves on the treadmill of working to live and living to work.

This ideology is disaster waiting to happen. Fear propels us—fear of not meeting expectations, at home and work, deadlines, performance goals. The fear of not being a great leader in our sector can hinder our performance. If we fear that our higher ups will be disappointed in our work, we may try even harder to succeed. Sometimes fear can cause a person to inflate realities or to gloss over a situation.

But that's not what a leader wants to hear or see. I guarantee you they want the truth. They would always prefer the truth. Truth is sustenance; leaders can work with the truth and develop needed outcomes. Being less than truthful dissipates the opportunity to accomplish excellence. Facing reality with the truth and replacing fear with faith allows for character building.

We need to let go of the fear that immobilizes rather than propels. We want to be propelled by traits that increase our success, like those exhibited by servant leaders and outlined in this book. If fear was ever the kindling that ignited the endeavors of great leaders, it was soon replaced by something more substantial, something more formidable to attaining lasting success. It is faith, as stated in Hebrews 11:1, that is the substance of things hoped for, the evidence of things not seen. Fear not, and go forward in faith leading with true servant leadership.

Rabbi Samuel E. Karff became Rabbi Emeritus of Congregation *Beth Israel in June of 1999. Now retired, he is on the Board of Directors of the Institute of Spirituality and Health at the Texas Medical Center. He is also a founding member of the Coalition of Criminal Justice.*

EVEN THE SPIRITUAL VIRTUOSO NEVER HAS IT MADE

Today, there is more spiritual openness in our country than 60 years ago when I was in college. Part of this hunger for the sacred is the result of disenchantment with modern substitutes for religious faith. I remember officiating at a baby naming ceremony for a family that had resettled in the U.S. from the Soviet Union. The father, taught to revere the icons of the communist state and to regard religion as a reactionary illusion, looked at his infant daughter and asked me, "Rabbi, do you believe in God?" When I replied "Yes," he responded, "I don't, but I hope she will."

Modernity has enthroned not only political ideology but technology as well. The modernist faith in technology is fueled by the hope of total dominion over nature, of being empowered to bend our world to our own selfish purposes. But as we live in the 21st century, we are sobered by a new sense of limits. Our assertion of dominion has posed the threat of ecological disaster.

There is also a growing awareness that the most profound answers to life's most important questions come not from science but religion. This increased openness to religion heightens both the perils and the opportunities for religious leaders.

Two historic examples illustrate the signs by which we can recognize perverted religious leadership. The first comes from the history of my own people. In the 17th century, a man named Shabbetai Tzevi claimed to be the long-awaited Jewish messiah. Many thousands of European Jews believed his claim, even when he violated basic moral and ritual requirements of the Torah. Even when, under pressure from the Turkish sultan, he abandoned Judaism altogether and converted to the sultan's religion—many did not cease to believe in him.

Tzevi, and some of the rabbis who supported his claim, justified his strange conduct in at least two ways: They claimed that he either had violated ordinary morality in the name of higher principles that had been revealed to him or, that yes, he did sin and that was the point—since a leader paradoxically must bring the community to redemption by his own immersion in sin. Was Shabbetai Tzevi a willful charlatan, or was he merely deluded? We do not know, but this much is certain—his perversion of spiritual leadership resulted in mass disillusionment within the European Jewish community.

Although of a different order of magnitude, the tragedy in Waco, Texas, twenty years ago also reveals the danger of perverted religious authority. David Koresh signed one of the last letters to his people with Hebrew script as "Koresh Adonai," which can be translated as, "Koresh is God." While presumably grounding his authority in Jewish and Christian scripture, he alone determined the norms by which the community and he, the leader, lived. Thus he separated husbands from wives, defined intimacy between husband and wife as adultery and intimacy between himself and any of the women (including eleven-and twelve-year-olds) as proper. He expropriated his followers' belongings and used their contributions to satisfy his whim for creature comforts and to amass an arsenal. He imposed his own system of social control, including corporal punishment and food deprivation.

Though there is much that separates the case of Shabbetai Tzevi from that of David Koresh, each exploited spiritual hunger and violated basic trust. From their example we can extrapolate two basic principles: 1) Beware of the religious leader who encourages for himself the adoration which should properly be focused on the One he is called to serve; 2) Beware of a religious leader who cavalierly violates deeply held religious norms or redefines what is permissible behavior in ways that obviously gratify his ego and impulses. A Tzevi, or a Koresh, illuminates by contrast what remains a paramount hallmark of responsible religious leadership: **the teacher must model the teaching**. As Martin Buber has written, "Either the teachings live in the life of a responsible human being or they are not alive at all."

Religious leaders have often been distinguished from their communities by burdens and privileges. Aaron the priest and his sons had special access to the symbols of worship. They presided over the altar and maintained the holy vessels. They accepted special sacred obligations and lived under certain conditions.

Religious leaders today are also often distinguished by cultic privileges and burdens. If they wear special attire, or stand some distance from the congregation in worship, or accept certain vows, which restrict their lives, those acts in themselves do not necessarily constitute holiness. Such actions may be temptations to self-adoration, manifestations for *yetzer hara*—the evil impulse. In rabbinic Judaism, temptation to evil focuses heavily on two sins. The first is idolatry, the worship of false gods, including oneself.

The sin of idolatry may be manifest in the leader's inclination to blur the distinction between God's and his own. Even Moses, perhaps the greatest religious leader in the history of Israel, was not immune to this temptation. Some medieval Jewish commentators regarded Moses' striking of the rock rather than speaking to it as God had, commanded as an instance in which Moses arrogated to himself and to Aaron the power of God. Before striking the rock Moses assembled and declared: "Listen, you rebels, is it from this rock that we have to produce water for you?" Here, said Nachmanides, is the core of Moses' sin. Here is why he was denied entry into the Promised Land. At that moment he saw himself not as an agent or servant of the Most High, but as the source of the miracle if water gushed from the rock.

If the first focus of the ancient rabbis' discussion of the *yetzer hara* is idolatry, the second is sexuality. A Talmudic tale frames the issue. When a certain rabbi observed a man and woman not married to each other walking down a wooded path he mused: "I must follow them and keep them from succumbing to the evil impulse." He observed them from a distance—and lo and behold, when they reached a fork in the road, they simply separated without having acted improperly.

The rabbi, far from feeling relieved, was troubled. He found himself thinking, "If I were in that man's place, I am not sure I would have been able to restrain my yetzer!" The rabbi found some comfort in the words of the prophet Elijah, who appeared and reminded him that, "The greater the man, the greater the yetzer." Translation: What makes you think that because you are a religious leader you should be above temptation? Far from it. The greater a person's learning, power, authority or charisma, the more energy he or she has for good or evil, and the greater the temptation to abuse that energy and power. *Even the spiritual virtuoso never has it made.*

As the Talmud insightfully notes, there is no area where the religious leader's modeling is more required, and none where the temptation to violate boundaries is more acute and devastating than sexuality. A person may turn to a religious leader in time of trouble seeking comfort in the teachings of faith, resources to cope with the darker side of life, a way to resist despair and assert that in spite of everything there is meaning. The religious leader who is cast as counselor mediates for the troubled person not only the teachings of the heritage but also the very presence of God. In such encounters the religious counselor is in the position of authority vis-à-vis a vulnerable, wounded person. That person needs to feel safe, able to speak honestly and expose pain without fear of exploitation. *In this context the greatest gift a leader can impart is trustworthiness.* Any betrayal of trust, any surrender to the yetzer is not only destructive to the person but alienates that person from his or her religious heritage, making less accessible the precious balm of faith when it is most needed.

The burden of modeling does not impose a standard of perfection. Even leaders are persons who stumble. And may there not be spiritual power in a leader who reveals his humanness, his vulnerability? The religious leader's personal share in the drama of confession, penitence, restitution and forgiveness is itself a hopeful model for the community he or she serves. It is unreasonable for members of a religious community to expect their leader never to disappoint them. No life and no person are without shadow.

What is true of our modeling of faith? A faith untouched by doubt or struggle is not a requirement of religious leadership. It may not even always be helpful. Elie Wiesel, who endured the horrors of the Holocaust and witnessed the death of his father in a camp, at first refused to say Kaddish, the prayer expressing praise of God in death as in life. Ultimately Wiesel recited the Kaddish, which (in an autobiographical novel) he calls, "That solemn affirmation filled with grandeur and serenity by which man returns to God his crown and his scepter."

Wiesel's confession of doubt and struggle and his refusal to abandon God have empowered him to help us remain sons and daughters of the covenant in a post-Holocaust world. Wiesel has said, "A Jew can be for God, with God, and even against God, but not without God."

But religious leaders need not model perfection in deed or creed, neither can they model moral frailty and lapses of faith. The communities they serve must discern that the teaching has made a profound and compelling difference in the quality of their leaders' lives. Especially in a post modern age where so many ideologies have been discredited, so much disenchantment has been endured, and so many leaders have failed, what we bring most compellingly to the task is our life—a life that credibly witnesses to the power of our professed faith.

That burden is considerably lighter when the leader confines himself to one-night stands—when the leader dazzles and mesmerizes and stirs the soul of listeners and then quickly moves on to another community. The burden is greater, far greater, when the leader lives with the community day after day, week after week, year after year. For then, the community comes to know the leader as well as his teaching.

This is the vocation of those in every tradition who are called not to be religious geniuses, not to found or radically reshape religious communities, but day by day to teach the faith, bring balm to the troubled, lead in worship, call a community to moral accountability and bring religious significance to the transitions of life.

Inspiration
FROM
Servant Leaders
IN
HoUSton
HEALTHCARE

Andrea White, *former first lady to Mayor Bill White, is a retired lawyer and author of four books of historical fiction for middle school readers, including the Bluebonnet List selection* Surviving Antarctica *(2006).*

DAILY MIRACLES

My best example:
Tony and Cynthia Petrello
and the glass building
they helped to build.
Drawing scientists from around the world
into collaborative spaces.
But it started, weighing only 584 grams.
A daughter, born early, named Carena,
much beloved.
Many questions when oxygen stops flowing to the brain.

No answers.
Cynthia's full time job—Carena.
Tony studied all the research.
Carena fought to stay here,
for a purpose.
Now parents from around the world
come to that glass building.
Carena—against all odds, walking, feeding herself;
She's fourteen years old,
the glass building—only two.
Many children will cross its doors,
some will find answers.

Cynthia and Tony Petrello's daughter, Carena, was born prematurely at 24 weeks, weighing a mere one pound four ounces. Carena was diagnosed with periventricular leukomalacia, a neurological disease of premature infants caused by a lack of oxygen to the brain. As a result, Carena developed cerebral palsy and other developmental delay issues.

There are many ways for people to respond, but Cynthia and Tony did what servant leaders do naturally, they viewed Carena's challenge as their own. Tony is a lawyer turned energy executive who earned scholarships to attend Yale for a math degree and Harvard for a law degree. He has a great mind, as well as a big heart and masterful management and research skills. Cynthia, a graduate of Albertus Magnus College, is a dancer turned actress turned full-time mom, possessed of both dignity and determination. Cynthia explains, "Dance taught me how to set and achieve goals."

Although the Petrellos received many different diagnoses for Carena, none of them included treatment for her underlying condition. As they searched for ways to help their only child Tony recognized, "an unmet need in health care for children with neurological disorders." He understood that complex problems required collaborative solutions; and Cynthia, who had spent years assembling a multi-disciplinary team to help Carena, was prepared to build an organization to help others.

With a nucleus of scientists from around the world, Cynthia and Tony started the Jan and Dan Duncan Neurological Research Institute at Texas Children's Hospital in Houston. The goal of the Institute, the first of its kind in the world, is to allow parents whose children receive a diagnosis of autism, epilepsy, cerebral palsy or other learning disability, to leave with a plan of treatment to help their child. With characteristic confidence, Cynthia and Tony embarked on the groundbreaking for the building before completing the massive task of fundraising. The facility opened in December 2010. As for Carena, because of the love, devotion and determination of her parents, the 14 year-old girl can walk with a walker, feed herself and perform other daily tasks. She possesses a few words and clearly says, "No." She loves music of all types, especially hip-hop and opera. Early odds would have been against these daily miracles.

"Carena is such a fighter," Cynthia says. "She works so hard for the things that all of us take for granted." The Petrellos were motivated to act because of something personal, but they knew others faced the same challenges and felt a responsibility to them. Just as they helped their own daughter, they are serving children around the world. Without the Petrellos and the generosity of Jan and Dan Duncan, the Neurological Institute would not exist.

Not all of us will undertake a service project that will have a global impact. But when we draw on our strengths and use them for a purpose beyond ourselves, we, in essence, become servant leaders. You never know what you will create, how big it will grow, or who you will help. But the potential is always enormous.

Houston is home to many world-class hospitals and research centers, all started by forward thinking individuals. I had never witnessed the birth of a medical institution before. The sight of the tall glass NRC building inspires me almost as much as Carena's story does. A photo of Carena smiling on the Petrello's holiday card this year reminds me of all that servant leadership can accomplish.

Linda K. May is Executive Director of the Simmons Foundation. The Founding Executive Director of the Women's Resource of Greater Houston, she currently serves on the boards of the Association of the Community Assistance, Coalition for the Homeless, and Homeless Youth Network, among others.

PHILANTHROPY'S ROLE—SUPPORTING MISSION-DRIVEN PASSION

Being involved in the philanthropic sector is an honor. Think of it—we are in the business of giving away money—other people's money. It's a privileged place, and program officers need to be mindful of the pitfalls that come with the territory and remain humble and approachable.

A grantor's first encounter with an agency is usually a request for funds. So it's easy to appreciate the susceptibility of program officers to become paternalistic and enjoy the role too much. To remain a servant in such an exalted position can be daunting. After all, a given agency's fate often lies in our hands because we're the ones who make the decision to fund or not to fund.

As our foundation matured, we grew in our understanding of how to relate to grantees. We quickly recognized that we wanted to be more than simply a vehicle for writing checks. Above all, we wanted to engage and partner with our grantees so we could understand their challenges, and join in the celebration of their successes. At the same time however, we realized that building such relationships does not happen quickly. It takes time to build trust. By creating an atmosphere of mutual respect, we have been able to minimize the gap of discomfort and wariness that often exists between funder and grantee. Our interactions needed to demonstrate that we shared the same objective—their success.

As grant-makers, we meet with fledgling and well-established organizations, and are exposed to all types and styles of leadership. We recognize that leaders in some organizations may not follow all the precepts of *servant leadership*. Yet, we often find committed and remarkable people involved at both the staff and board levels. They may not know the term *servant leadership*, or be aware of its implications, but they have the skill, determination and the dedication to lead their respective agencies with all the sensitivities of a true servant leader.

The would-be endgame is always the same—to help the underserved obtain, among other things, a healthy lifestyle; the ability to live independently and master any behavioral problems; workplace readiness with meaningful, fulfilling work; an education; and to gain the capacity of successfully managing his or her mental health.

Healthcare for the Homeless' Houston Chapter represents one of the best examples of the kind of organization in which philanthropists want to invest their time, energy and funds. Dr. David Buck, its founder, is one of the finest examples of servant leadership in action. Examining Dr. Buck's life trajectory is an exercise in determination and mission-driven values. After graduating from college David applied to medical school. While his application was being processed over a series of months, he went to India, where he labored alongside Mother Theresa in Calcutta witnessing unbelievable poverty and illness. As hard as he worked however, he was always an outsider. Throughout his stay he was repeatedly told, "You're not from here," implying that, culturally, he wasn't able to understand or minister to India's sick and infirm.

While in India David learned his application to medical school had been rejected. Disappointment, coupled with the realization that the attitudes of the people he was trying to help were deeply rooted, David returned to the U.S. where culture would not separate him from those he wanted to serve—the poor and disenfranchised. Undaunted, he reapplied to medical school and, simultaneously, applied and was accepted to the University of Texas' masters program at the School of Public Health.

Not long after he began his master's degree in Public Health (MPH), he learned his recent application to medical school had in fact been accepted. David fast-tracked his MPH, finishing the two-year program in nine months and entered medical school even before he had completed his master's degree. As part of his MPH, he helped establish two free clinics at Casa Juan Diego, where there was little healthcare available in the surrounding community.

And his legacy began.

Although David was aware that his medical career was going to be untraditional, he did not know what form it would take. After graduation, he did his residency in Rochester, New York. While there, he observed and was disturbed by the barriers to healthcare for the underserved. He later moved to Colorado and worked at a nonprofit clinic, which subsequently became a Federally Qualified Health Center (FQHC) that he helped establish. After several years of rural practice, he was recruited by the Baylor College of Medicine and moved back to Houston. It was then that he came face-to-face with the full extent of homelessness and the barriers to healthcare in the community in which he had been raised.

David felt a deep connection between himself and the people in his community who have led such difficult lives, with little hope or dignity. As he became more familiar with those whose lives were spent on the streets, he began to understand the pattern of homelessness, which manifested itself, in many cases, in those who went from jail to the street to the hospital to the street and, again, back to jail.

The Harris County Hospital District had done a study, concluding that the homeless were ten times more likely to be re-admitted for healthcare than were the poor who *were* housed. So, in 1999, Dr. Buck began *Healthcare for the Homeless* (HHH), ministering to those same people he saw daily, living on the streets. His idea was to bring them the very things they lacked—quality healthcare, hope and dignity, revitalizing them in body, mind and spirit. Watching David minister to the homeless is an inspiring experience. He listens, examines, watches and then listens some more. Each person is given the attention and care he or she deserves as a fellow human being.

In order to reach as many homeless individuals as possible, HHH partnered with some 30 agencies that included homeless shelters and day centers. HHH is now a Federally Qualified Health Center, and delivering primary care; however, the FQHC quickly recognized the need to provide dental care as well. Interestingly enough, there are before and after photos of the dental patients. The look on the faces of those who now have dentures, clean teeth and a winning smile says everything. They are filled with pride, not embarrassment, and there is no fear of rejection based on their appearance when they open their mouths to apply for a job. All one can see is the promise of a different future.

As he saw the differences in the lives of those who came to HHH, David wanted to do even more. To that end, in 2006, HHH established a jail in-reach program that helps prevent the jail to street to jail pattern previously described. To prevent this cycle from continuing, HHH starts to work with offenders before they are released. And upon release, a representative from HHH meets them, assists them in getting their medications and connects them with resources that provide basic needs, such as food, shelter and clothing. This program alone has reduced the re-arrest rate by 64 percent!

In keeping with David's philosophy of encouraging colleagues to continue serving the underserved throughout their careers, he launched the Houston-Galveston chapter of the Albert Schweitzer Fellowship Program in 2009. This competitive program is available to students enrolled in disciplines such as medicine, law, engineering and social work that express an interest in public service. The Fellowship is an effort to develop *Leaders in Service*—individuals who are dedicated to addressing the healthcare needs of underserved communities, who understand that this work is a lifetime journey and who have the potential to influence and inspire others by example.

During their 200 hours of direct service, the Fellows work tirelessly to address healthcare disparities throughout the region. Listening to them describe their projects, the lessons learned, the community members helped and the joy derived from working collaboratively with their partner agency, is to realize that servant leadership is alive and well in the next generation. Their projects have impacted a wide range of people—refugees, the elderly and the homeless young adults, and issues such as childhood obesity diabetes. The Fellows' creativity in developing programs has been astonishing, and it's clear that these experiences in particular will have a lasting impact throughout their lives.

David Buck has instilled within the Schweitzer participants the desire to stay closely connected to the community in which they live and work. As a result, his legacy will reach well beyond his lifetime, and will impact the greater Houston region for as long as there is an underserved population that needs attention and quality healthcare.

In summary, servant leadership is not a label or a catch phrase. It can be understood best by examining its impact on individual lives and its effect, for example, on the future health of a community. Dr. Buck is the quintessential servant leader—determined, skillful, reflective, selfless, caring, enterprising, wise and mission-driven. Due to his inspiration and influence, David has become, unintentionally, one of our community's greatest assets.

The Simmons Foundation is both humbled and proud to have been given the opportunity to partner with HHH and the Schweitzer program in an effort to improve healthcare outcomes for the underserved in our community, and to help fulfill the mission of a visionary servant leader—David Buck, M.D., MPH.

Dr. Lovell A. Jones *is Director of the Dorothy I. Height Center for Health Equity and Evaluation Research; Office of the Vice President for Cancer Prevention & Population Sciences; Director of the Reproductive Biology Program, The University of Texas, Houston; and Professor at MD Anderson and the University of Houston.*

EVENTS HAVE A WAY OF SHAPING ONE'S LIFE

As I look over my life as a servant leader, a great deal of the basis for this side of my personality can be found in the influence my great-grandmother had on my grandmother, and then in her impact on my mother and aunts. If it were not for my grandmother and my aunts working to support my mother's efforts to go to college, I probably would not be where I am today. Each was a leader in their respective communities, but each never aspired to be a leader first. What they all instilled in me was a desire to help those less fortunate than myself. Each of these women also had a significant event occur during her life that altered its direction.

In the late seventies, an event involving my mother forever changed the direction of my life. However, before getting there, other events took place that shaped my life as well. Growing up, I felt that I was placed on this earth for a purpose that was greater than what I could ever imagine. And it seemed everything that occurred pushed me in that direction. As a young boy, I was enrolled in what is now known as a charter school. Southern University Laboratory School was a school for African-Americans that one took an exam to get into. After finishing McKinley Elementary I entered Southern Lab. However, the only way of getting to school from where I lived was to take a bus that transported college students. Those morning and evening rides introduced me to the idea of political activism. From there, I was among the first African-Americans to integrate schools in Baton Rouge. To be instilled with the idea that you are setting a path for others to follow is a breath-taking endeavor. I could, and probably should, write more about this part of my life, but the intent of opening with this is to explain the basis for my journey in becoming a servant leader.

At no point in my life did I aspire to be a leader first, but rather, I wanted to provide a path for others to follow, to provide an environment so they too could have the best opportunity to achieve their goals. A number of years and events transpired between my days at Robert E. Lee High School and my first day at the University of California Berkeley— moving to California, getting married, having my first child and then graduating from college. During my years at Berkeley, I helped to build one of the most successful minority recruitment programs in the country. The individuals recruited are now leaders in their own right.

In 1977, I started my National Institutes of Health postdoctoral fellowship at the University of California San Francisco Medical Center. As a molecular endocrinologist, I knew I would be working in one of the leading reproductive endocrinology groups in the country. In December 1978, my mother came for a visit. It should have struck me as strange, but I was so excited to have my mother visit and to see where her son would soon be working—I was well on my way to being offered a faculty position. My wife had landed her dream job teaching at the San Francisco Unified School District, and everything seemed to be on track. I remember my wife saying to me, "Something is wrong with your mother." I ignored the comment. Then, in May 1979, I received a fateful call that changed my life.

The reason for my mother's visit in December 1978 was to say good-bye. You see, my mother was diagnosed with breast cancer and thought that she was going to die. Here I was a breast cancer researcher who was on his way to the top of his field, and my mother thought that cancer was an automatic death sentence. It was then that I made the decision to leave my comfort zone and head to the number one cancer center in America, the University of Texas MD Anderson Cancer Center, then known as the University of Texas MD Anderson Research & Tumor Institute. I did not know how I was going to be hired, but that is where I was headed. Ultimately, my mentor was offered a job as chair of a new department at MD Anderson, the Department of Molecular Endocrinology. And as they say, the rest is history.

The desire to be a servant leader comes from a natural feeling that one wants to serve first. That inclination is a conscious choice that sometimes inspires one to assume a leadership role. Well, I came to MD Anderson to change the face of cancer so that others diagnosed with breast cancer would not feel they were given a death sentence. It was not to start a national meeting on addressing health disparities, or to co-found the largest multicultural health policy organization, or later, to lead an effort into developing a joint venture between the University of Houston, and the University of Texas and MD Anderson. It was to do what was innate in me—be a servant leader—though I didn't know what to call it at the time.

My mentor used to say, "One's legacy to science is not the work that you do but the people you leave behind." To me this is just another ex-ample of a servant leader. Over the years, I have taken this to heart. I have been told that the difference between one who is just a leader and one who is a servant leader manifests itself in the care taken by the ser-vant—it is first to make sure that other people's highest priority needs are being met. Over the years, since coming to MD Anderson Cancer Center, I have tried to emulate what my mentor instilled in me. I have been told that a true servant leader is one who offers an inclusive vision; one who views most situations from a more integrated, holistic position; one who listens carefully to others as well as shows empathy; one who persuades through reason; has the foresight to understand the lessons from the past, the realities of the present and the likely consequence of a decision for the future; one who has the stewardship to serve the needs of others and heal divisions while building community.

As a servant leader, change has been at the heart of my efforts. As I stated earlier, I came to MD Anderson to change the face of cancer. And in doing so, I evolved into a servant leader. Change is not always easy. Dr. Martin Luther King Jr. once said, "Change does not roll in on the wheels of inevitability, but comes through continuous struggle." That struggle for change bears fruit when we seek to serve others first, to find common ground, to use power ethically and to insist on fairness and equality. Dr. Dorothy I. Height once said, "If you worry about who is going to get credit, you don't get much work done," and that, "Greatness is not measured by what a man or woman accomplishes, but by the opposition he or she has overcome to reach certain goals."

More than 30 years later, after my move to Houston, the test of whether I evolved into a successful servant leader would be determined by a number of factors: Had those who had been with me grown? Had the community I'd served become healthier, wiser, freer, more autonomous and more likely themselves to become servants? And, what had been the effect on the underserved in Houston during my years here, had they benefitted from my efforts?

And finally, as my mentor once said, "Your legacy will be the people you have left behind to continue to work toward health equity—." *That* is servant leadership.

Jana Mullins served for many years as a Program Officer for the Rockwell Fund, Inc., a nonprofit foundation in Houston, and is the author of Open Hands: Lessons on Giving and Receiving. *She currently works at The Brookwood Community for functionally disabled adults.*

JOURNEY OF A SERVANT LEADER

Maria's journey began in 1990 with this statement: "We've decided to go to the U.S. and we're leaving tomorrow. Do you want to come?"

"She must be kidding. I can't do that!" ran through Maria's mind. However, from somewhere deep inside, a voice within her gave a resounding *"YES!"*

She was nineteen years old. Life for Maria, her parents and her seven siblings was more than difficult. Since moving to San Miguel de Allende following the Mexico City earthquake, they had barely enough to get by. Only days before she held her crying baby and wondered, with tears streaming down her face, where she, as a single mother, would find the money to feed them both. That evening Maria would tell her parents she had made the decision to go to the United States in search of work to help support them. She would send money home, she promised.

The next day, she would leave her baby daughter in her parents' care, and step out the door with nothing more than a small bag, the clothes on her back and the tiny amount of money her parents had given her for the trip. Maria, her two friends and a "coyote" who had been hired by her friend's family to bring them to the U.S., began their walk to Juarez, Mexico. After hours of walking, they finally reached Juarez only to be stopped by Immigration. Maria's two friends were told to go back, they would not be allowed to cross. For reasons Maria will never know, they allowed her and the "coyote" woman to continue. They arrived at the airport where the "coyote" purchased two one-way tickets to Houston. Maria realized there was no turning back. Landing in Houston they took a bus to the north side, where Maria would begin her new life. She was taken to a home to work as a housekeeper, where she was essentially held as a slave. Locked inside during the day and never allowed to leave, she was given only scraps of food from other people's plates. At night, she was taken to an office building that she was meant to clean. The salary promised for all the cleaning and cooking was never paid. Maria was forbidden to speak to anyone, and to ensure her silence the woman who employed her threatened to report Maria to authorities for stealing.

Months later, a couple came to visit the woman and witnessed the abuse suffered by Maria. When Maria's employer left the room, the couple asked Maria if she would like their help to leave her current situation. Maria couldn't say yes fast enough. The next day when the woman was not home, the couple returned to rescue Maria. She was taken to their home where she was treated with dignity and respect.

My journey began the summer of 1993. This was the same summer my path and Maria's would cross. And it was at this intersection that the seeds of service and servant leadership were initially sown. Maria knocked on my door, and when I opened it I saw a sweet, petite twenty-one-year-old standing there. While she did not speak a word of English, in that moment, unbeknownst to each other, God would send us on an unforgettable journey that would bind us to each other for the rest of our lives. A year later I found myself in a similar position as Maria—a single mother, raising three young children, going back to school at the age of forty and beginning a new life. When I went back to college and started working full time Maria cared for my children after school and took English and computer classes at night. In those years there were many times when the seeds of service and servant leadership would again be sown between us. Maria was my encourager and my supporter as I began a new career and rebuilt my life.

There were days when I would provide that same encouragement and support to her as she was learning a new language and studying for her GED. After months and months of studying, her hard work paid off and she earned her degree. Maria, never without a goal, then enrolled at Houston Community College, attending classes five nights a week to earn her associate's degree. She volunteered during the day at a women's nonprofit organization where she assisted other women, many of them single mothers who had also been in a similar situation in Mexico.

By helping others, Maria discovered that she was also helping herself. In her quiet, confident way, she began taking a leadership role in the organization and within her community. She started by heading up the food and clothing drives, by teaching classes and most importantly, by making herself available in her community for those other women who needed her. She listened to them, helped them find the resources they needed and along the way, encouraged them to go to school so they too could get better jobs, support their families and grow to become the very best women they had the potential to be. Maria was a servant leader in every degree. I would often visit Maria during my lunch hour or when she worked on the weekends and was amazed at the difference she was making in these women's lives. She served and affirmed them, and the strong, supportive leadership she provided gave them a foundation to enact servant leadership in their endeavors as well.

As the years went by and my children became more independent, entering high school and going off to college, Maria, now in her thirties, graduated from Houston Community College with her associate's degree. Shortly thereafter, she became one of the first *Certified Community Health Workers*, or *Promotoras* in our city. It was also during this time Maria began studying for her citizenship exam and embarked on the long and arduous process of becoming a U.S. citizen. It would be years before she would take her oath and the dream of becoming an American citizen materialized.

A few months later, UTMB Galveston was awarded a federal grant to implement an innovative community health theater project. Through the nonprofit organization Maria then worked for, she was asked to take the lead and help develop this program. This project ultimately led Maria to her life's passion and the pursuit of her bachelor's degree at the University of Houston-Downtown.

Working in community theater and health education, she began encouraging individuals in disadvantaged neighborhoods to write and act in their neighborhood plays. These plays were about health issues people faced in their neighborhoods, including lead poisoning, obesity, asthma and cancer. Maria educated people on how to prevent these diseases and make healthier lifestyle choices. Maria's servant leadership helped guide individuals who never would have dreamed of participating in a play, much less of standing up and expressing themselves in public. In turn, through their involvement they would help their neighbors live healthier, happier and more productive lives.

After numerous community health plays were produced, it was proven that this model of health education was making a difference. The plays educated and empowered people to take control of their health and their lives. In fact, they were so successful that Maria was asked to speak on Spanish television and radio multiple times and to write a chapter in a book about the effectiveness of this model within the community. She was also asked by a physician at UTMB Galveston to accompany him to Colombia, South America, to produce a community health play with the local people, demonstrating to community leaders how to produce their own plays and empower their community to seek healthier solutions.

After Maria returned from Colombia she was offered a position as a Community Health Liaison, a position she holds to this day. Maria is living out her passion—promoting community health education.

In December 2010, after I had the treasured gift of watching each one of my children graduate from college with their own personal strengths and persistence, I would receive one more remarkable and precious gift: The gift of watching one of the most extraordinary women I know, at the age of forty, after twenty arduous years of working full time, serving others by day and attending college at night, achieve her dream of receiving her bachelor's degree. As she walked across the stage in her cap and gown, a mature woman full of confidence and grace, to receive both her hard-earned and heart-earned degree, I recalled in that moment the sweet, petite twenty-one-year-old who first stood at my door, unable to speak a word of English. It had been an unforgettable, twenty-year,

God-sent journey. This journey had its ups and downs, its challenges and its rewards—for both of us. But this journey was full of knowledge, warmth, growth and servant leadership.

How does an individual grow to become a servant leader?

"We must be silent before we can listen. We must listen before we can learn. We must learn before we can prepare. We must prepare before we can serve. We must serve before we can lead." – **William Arthur Ward**

No matter who we are or where we come from, we all are born with the seeds of greatness and a servant's heart. It is our choice however, whether we will choose to listen to our heart, take a courageous step, and like Maria, humbly walk the path to help others and lead each other to success, wherever life's endeavors may lead.

Inspiration
FROM
Servant Leaders
IN
HOUSTON
COMMUNITY

Chris Bell has been practicing law in Texas for more than twenty years in a litigation firm that primarily focuses on Houston and the surrounding area; he was elected to the United States Congress in 2002, and returned to the courtroom in 2009.

THE PARK IN A NIGHT PROJECT

When I had the privilege of serving in the United States Congress, groups of young people would often visit the Capitol. I always tried to make it as interesting for them as possible, and to leave them with something they could remember. When they would ask about my thoughts on public service, I would share one of my favorite stories about a very successful Houston lawyer. This lawyer had made countless sums of money but always seemed to find himself in very controversial situations; he was often accused of trying to land new cases by unethical means. On one occasion, a newspaper profile was written about the lawyer. One of his colleagues was asked why someone would act as such after making so much money. The colleague replied, "There's no amount of money in the world that would ever fill the hole in his life."

I thought it was a powerful quote and I have never forgotten it. I would share it with the young people, not to lead them to believe money is somehow evil, but to teach them a lesson about fulfillment. For me, public service filled the hole in my life like nothing else ever could. I would tell those young folks that if they could ever find anything in their lives that could really "fill the hole" and bring them that sense of fulfillment, grab on to that like nothing before and never let go.

I believe it's that sense of fulfillment that leads to true servant leadership; if you are fulfilled, you most likely love what you are doing. And if you love and enjoy what you are doing, you are going to be a lot better at it. There is also a strong possibility that you are doing it for the right reasons, not for great personal glory but to build a better community.

That's one of the great misunderstandings about public service today, especially those who serve the public through elected office. Politics has taken on such a negative connotation with so many in this day and age that it's nearly impossible for most to imagine that anything positive could possibly come from it. But that's because negative stories about politics and politicians dominate the mainstream media and one rarely sees stories about elected officials doing the right thing for the right reasons. But believe me, during my years in politics, I saw plenty of examples and, based on my personal experience, those are the examples that demonstrate why public service is so worthwhile.

My favorite story, and perhaps best example of what I'm talking about, involves a park renovation project. I think it teaches a lot about community, opportunity and leadership. Back in 1997, I had just been elected to the Houston City Council, and I happened to read an article about a project in another country called, "Park in a Night." Leaders in the community had identified a vacant square block in a neighborhood in desperate need of green space. After recruiting a lot of volunteers, receiving a lot of donations of talent, equipment and materials, they put together a plan to go in army-style and, in one night, turn that blighted square block into a little park. The purpose was twofold: provide the neighborhood with more park space, but also send a message that such positive change was possible—sometimes even overnight.

The "Park in a Night" project was a huge success, and the concept fascinated me. However, I wasn't sure how such an idea could be made to work in Houston. Then an opportunity presented itself. I had been asked to join the 1997 class of Leadership Houston, a local organization that brings in leaders from all different walks of life to learn more about the city and what makes it tick. As part of the eight-month course, every Leadership Houston class is asked to select a group project, something in which every member of the class can participate. That's when it hit me. Why not a project similar to the "Park in a Night" project? The volunteer problem would be solved because of the man-and woman-power already in the group. And, as for finding the right space and getting some materials and equipment, I felt certain I could do that because of my position on City Council.

It soon became clear that we would have to take a different approach to finding the right property because we weren't in a position to buy a vacant lot. Someone on my City Council staff suggested that we look for a city park that had fallen into disrepair and try to bring it back to life. I thought that sounded like a great approach and asked the staff member to begin the search. We ended up finding the perfect place rather quickly.

Baldwin Park had been around forever, but it was obvious that it had originally been surrounded by vibrant neighborhoods. Over time, residents had moved out and people going to the park looking to buy and use drugs had moved in. But new homes were beginning to be built in the area and those moving in would be looking for green space. What they would find at Baldwin Park was no playground—a lonesome, rusted swing-set, basketball goals with no nets and no playing field whatsoever. Furthermore, the old fountain in the park had become a trash receptacle, and there was so much debris in the grass that it was dangerous to walk barefoot.

We had found our space! Working with my fellow Leadership Houston members and City of Houston officials, we came up with a plan. It would not be as auspicious as the "Park in a Night" plan, but if it all worked out, it could be just as meaningful to the neighborhood. Leadership Houston would have to do its part by providing the volunteers to clear away the very large amount of trash and debris and by purchasing a large piece of playground equipment. The City of Houston Parks Department agreed to put in a new soccer field and fix the equipment already there, such as the swing-set and basketball goals. All of this would take place over a few days in the spring of 1998.

It could not have gone any better. Everyone did their part; Leadership Houston volunteers descended upon the park early one Saturday and engaged in a massive clean up. We didn't know how much broken glass we would encounter when we got there, but luckily it was concentrated in one area and we were able to pick most of it out of the grass, even though it was quite tedious. We also cleared trash from the fountain and other parts of the park along with overgrown brush. Later, the city came in to place the new playground equipment in a newly built safe space surrounded by sand. The swing-set was painted and a soccer field with nets was put in place where before there was nothing but an old back-stop. In an incredibly short period of time, Baldwin Park had taken on a whole new look and feel.

The park was not on my regular route home from work, but one evening about a month after the big clean-up day I decided I would drive by just to take a look. As I got close, I saw a very different place: there was a woman with her baby sitting on a bench; there were kids playing on the new piece of equipment and others swinging on the renovated swing-set, and there were bigger kids running up and down the soccer field. The once inner city wasteland had been transformed. It was now actually productive green space that added immeasurable significance to the neighborhood.

At that moment, I realized that I had been part of something for which there would never be a dollar value, something that had left me with a feeling that I would never be able to completely explain. It was that moment that left me absolutely no doubt that success and fulfillment in public service would always be measured in a completely different way than it was in other walks of life. In that moment, I could not have felt any better about what we had done or any greater sense of value or accomplishment. To have been able to take an idea and then work with others to build it into a reality, a reality that would leave a neighborhood better than it had been before, and residents with more sense of pride than they had before, was absolutely incredible—and in many ways indescribable.

And that's all there was to it. It was just that indescribably great feeling. No news stories. Really, no publicity whatsoever. No big dedication ceremony or public accolades. It was just that feeling of servant leadership, of having led an act of service that made an immeasurable difference in your community. And it was so much more than enough.

Vanessa **Gilmore,** *United States District Judge of the Southern District of Texas, serves as a member of the Board of Trustees for Hampton University and on the board of Inprint.*

HELP FOR THE CHILDREN OF INCARCERATED PARENTS

I have served as a United States district judge for eighteen years. For many of those years, when I sentenced criminal defendants, I recited the standard verbiage about the reasons for the particular sentence to be imposed—that the sentence satisfied the objectives of punishment, deterrence and incapacitation. Somewhere along the path to justice however, the focus on rehabilitation seemed to have been lost. There was never any thought given to what incarceration might do to a defendant's family. That was not our concern. But it should have been.

Seventy-five percent of children whose parents are incarcerated end up incarcerated themselves. At some point I had to ask myself what role I, as judge, could play to interrupt the pipeline from the cradle to prison. Didn't my service require that I love justice and do mercy? I began to pay attention to the children of the incarcerated—statistical data that we usually don't collect. It was no surprise to find that almost all of the defendants we sentenced had children. But these children were not part of the criminal justice system, at least not yet, so we paid them no mind.

I began to realize that the value of a leadership position was the opportunity to use it for good. It was at that time that my journey began to try to find a way to reach past the men and women who stood before me for sentencing, and to reach out to their children and say, "You don't have to take this path." I took advantage of opportunities to speak to "troubled" children and found, not surprisingly, that the majority of them had lost one or both parents to incarceration. At one middle school I spoke to a group of fifty such girls, all of whom had at least one parent in prison. Many were angry, depressed, ashamed and often bitter about their situation. Most were living with grandparents or other caretakers who were ill-equipped financially and/or emotionally to deal with these children's losses. Most importantly, recognizing and dealing with the emotional needs *always* took a back seat to day-to-day survival.

I also realized that many of the caretakers just did not have any idea how to start helping these kids recover from the emotional devastation of their loss and help them to choose a different path from the ones their parent(s) had chosen. That is how *A Boy Named Rocky* was born, a book for the children of incarcerated parents. Together with my co-author, psychotherapist Dr. Janice Beal, we wrote a book to provide parents, caretakers, educators, counselors and mental health professionals with a way to begin a healing dialogue with children about their losses.

A Boy Named Rocky was produced as a coloring book, because coloring is often used as an icebreaker to help children open up about issues that affect them. Because of that, we initially thought the book would primarily appeal to younger children. Surprisingly, however, the book also appealed to adolescents, older teenagers and even adults, many of whom told us that no one had ever helped them address the very real hurt, loss and shame they suffered from losing a parent through incarceration. The book seeks to address those issues in a simple, easy to read story about one young boy named Rocky. It provides children with tools for understanding their parents are not bad people; they are people who made bad choices. It suggests ways the children can get help, so they can in turn make better choices. It also helps children to express their own feelings, even providing a form letter they can use to write to their parents. Part of the message is also to the incarcerated parents, because it encourages them to take responsibility for helping their children choose a different, and more positive, path for their own lives.

Originally, I thought the book would just be something that I could share with churches and other community organizations that worked with this population of children. And in fact, *Big Brothers Big Sisters* of Texas decided to incorporate the book into their Amachi program for the children of incarcerated parents, allowing us to reach thousands of children across the state of Texas. Still, I was searching for a way to reach the children of the people who passed through the doors of our courthouse. Fortunately, that opportunity presented itself when I was asked to use my book as part of a new program developed by our pre-trial services officers to educate our defendants about the various programs we had available to them and their families while they were on pre-trial release. Finally I had an opportunity to bring together my roles as judge, author and mother to talk to our defendants about taking advantage of resources for them and their children, including the opportunity to receive family counseling and treatment.

I initially wondered how well our defendants would receive the message that they should stop worrying about their own situations and focus their attention and what time they had left before incarceration on the future well being of their children. The message was amazingly well received, and as a result we began to have more success assisting the families of our defendants. What we found out, however, was that many of the defendants had a myriad of legal problems that could not be handled by their criminal lawyers. That motivated me to ask the dean of the Thurgood Marshall School of Law at Texas Southern University to come to one of our programs to see the work we were doing. As a result, the dean agreed to begin a legal clinic at the law school specifically to help our defendants address problems that would benefit their children and families prior to their incarceration. The U.S. Pre-trial Legal Clinic has assisted our defendants and their families with a variety of matters, including social security, landlord and tenant, guardianships and wills.

I now get regular requests from our pre-trial services officers for copies of *A Boy Named Rocky*, which I happily provide at my expense because I recognize that leadership requires service. While I may not be able to do anything to help the people who stand before me, by reaching past them to help their children I have the chance to interrupt the pipeline from cradle to prison, and help their children choose a better path.

The other incidental benefit for all of us is the very real chance of reducing recidivism or re-incarceration by giving our defendants real hope that they will have a healthy, happy family to return to after they complete their period of incarceration.

The price of keeping a federal inmate imprisoned for one year: $27,000; keeping just one child from following their parent into prison—priceless.

Khambrel Marshall *is a member of the KPRC Local 2 Severe Weather Team and host of* Houston Newsmakers with Khambrel Marshall. *He sits on the Board of Directors of the YMCA of Greater Houston and the March of Dimes, Texas Gulf Coast. Additionally, he is a trustee for Goodwill Industries of Houston and is a Senior Fellow in the American Leadership Forum.*

A MOTHER'S SMILE

"A Mother's Smile is Something Special." That was the title of an essay I wrote in 1984 after my mother died of cancer. It was a tribute to her and recalled the last time in her life that she smiled. I was blessed to have been there to see it. That beautiful, wide smile that lit up any room she entered was, for a final time, directed at me as I walked into her San Francisco hospital room. It had been a long trip from Connecticut. I had come at the urging of my father, who a day earlier, had called and said, "I think you should come. It doesn't look good." She called my name and asked why I was there. I joked that I heard she was giving the nurses a hard time and that I was there to help them out. She smiled that beautiful, wide Francetta Cole Marshall trademark smile and settled back in her bed. She never smiled again.

For the next few days she slipped further into delirium. Her last hours triggered the beginning of a deep introspection that ultimately led to my declaration for a lifelong commitment to servant leadership... before I'd ever heard the phrase.

My mother, by her example, began building that servant leadership foundation in me when I was very young. She was honest to a fault and sincerely cared about those around her.

My father was also influential, even while his thirty-year commitment serving our country in the U.S. Army often led to long stretches away from home, leaving the very delicate human construction project in my mother's hands.

I watched my mother care and reach out to help people in our neighborhood and church. I was amazed at how she was able to encourage others to find paths to success when they otherwise seemed unsure. Our house always seemed to have several more teenagers than the ones who actually lived there. They were attracted to an environment I took for granted, where there was always much laughter and more than enough love to go around. I didn't know it then, but my mother was teaching us lessons we would use for the rest of our lives.

From her I learned to not just *say* I love someone, but that I have to *show* it. It is the best way by far to gain someone's confidence and faith in you—by letting them see the confidence and faith you have in them. When I think back to the special smile that was ever present in my life, I can't help but be thankful for the teamwork my parents put forth to help light my pathway to and through adulthood.

"If a job is first begun, never quit until it's done. If that job is big or small, do it well or not at all."

I must have heard my father say those sentences hundreds, if not thousands of times. He repeated them for effect. Every night of my young life, I went to bed with the smell of Kiwi shoe polish and Brasso in my nostrils. It was my father preparing for his next day, to take on his next job, big or small, looking spit-shined and clean while doing it. Francetta and Cambrel Marshall instilled in me a strong drive to want to make a difference. To see all problems as solvable, with the right plan and right people in place and with the persistence and patience to see it through. My parents also taught me to learn from my mistakes.

I was the President of the German Club in Junior High. I was not a German language student. The German Club advisor was not happy. I resigned. Lesson learned? Just because someone will follow, it does not mean I'm the best person to lead the way.

At my high school in Seaside California, my actions led to the institution of the *Minor Mistake of the Year* award after I competed in a Drum Major competition. After it was over, I discovered that my zipper was wide open the entire time! Lesson learned? Overlooking even the smallest detail can lead to big problems later.

In my thirty-seven years in the television business, I have always worked to make a difference in the communities in which our family has lived. I once believed my motivation for doing it was because it was good business for my station. Early in my career, during a contract negotiation, I decided to make a point by stopping my volunteer activities on behalf of the station. It lasted only a few weeks. Lesson learned? Serving your community in any capacity means putting your heart and soul into something you care about. Caring is not a trait that can be turned off.

Before moving to Houston I would never have put this city on a list of places I'd prefer to live. My mistake. Once I arrived, I discovered a big city with a small town charm and warmth from people who seemed to have never met a stranger. It is a community of native Houstonians, joined by the rest of us who "got here as soon as we could" and have determined to make a difference in the lives of so many who need our help. As one of those Houstonians, I have been blessed to work with and take leadership roles with some tremendous organizations that have made positive impacts throughout Southeast Texas. I would like to acknowledge some of those Servant Leader organizations:

Big Brothers Big Sisters of Southeast Texas: I took over as Chairman at a time when the organization was having severe money, among other, problems. Very tough decisions had to be made about restructuring, and it validated the importance of fiduciary responsibility of board members. Our decisions have a real impact on the lives of those who depend on our organizations for their salaries. I lost many nights of sleep worrying about the ramifications of the tough decisions I, and my board, would have to make. To see that organization now thriving, as part of *Big Brothers Big Sister Lone Star*, the largest *Big Brothers Big Sisters* board in the country, is a wonderful reward for the hard work of a dedicated few who personified the values of servant leadership.

The Collaborative for Children: This board was incredible as we fought to gain traction for support of early childhood education, trying to convince legislators and funders that putting financial support into programs that help shape the young minds of the children in our community is money very well spent.

The March of Dimes, Texas Gulf Coast: My involvement with this organization has also been an incredible experience. Men and women have dedicated their lives to making sure our babies are not born prematurely; and because of research done with money we raise, the children who are born too soon and too small have a better chance of surviving.

I was honored to have been Chairman of the 2011 March for Babies in Houston, the largest walk in the United States for the March of Dimes, with more than 45,000 people who helped raise more than three-and-a-half million dollars! Thousands of servant leaders who had a vision drew up plans and started neighborhood teams that walked five miles for a life saving cause.

The YMCA of Greater Houston: This is the largest child-care provider in Houston. As Chairman of the marketing committee, I have been blessed to be surrounded by some of the smartest marketing people I know. They are all servant leader volunteers who bring their ideas and talents to the table to help us enrich the lives of children, seniors and families.

The *American Leadership Forum of Houston*: This group exemplifies all of the qualities of servant leadership. The ALF helped teach me collaborative techniques and principles that have changed my life. My Class XXIII experience taught me how to truly listen to other points of view in order to become a better leader, husband and father, and I will forever be grateful for the privilege of getting to know and watch servant leaders in action.

The common denominator among all of these organizations has been the amazing synergy created when men and women from all faiths and occupations come together, bring to the table confidence in who they are, have a vision for the right thing to do and a willingness to lead, follow or work as a team to achieve success for the greater good.

As a little boy in Junction City, Kansas, on the wall of a Baptist church I once saw a sign that helped shape my life. It read, "If everyone in this church were just like me, what kind of church would this church be?"

Substitute the word community for church and the answer is my call to action. Volunteer, lead, sacrifice, care and never ever give up. It is my lifelong commitment, one for which I need no pay or thanks.

My mother's smile is enough.

Bonnie Crane Hellums *is a 247th District Court Judge, a Licensed Professional Counselor, a Licensed Marriage and Family Therapist and an Advanced Addiction Counselor.*

REBUILDING FAMILIES

I never dreamed that I would do with my life what I have done. I was brought up in a church-going family by a mother who strongly believed in giving back through her numerous charities and service organizations in addition to her church work. I started out wanting to be a high school counselor, but found out as I graduated from SMU, with degrees in religion and psychology, I would have to teach for years first, and that the two fields I could teach were not offered in high school. So I opted for graduate school. At the University of Illinois I earned a masters in Counseling and Guidance, and Rehabilitation Counseling and Higher Education Administration. Through all this, I was gaining knowledge about myself and walking through life trying to understand who my father was. He was a pilot in WWII; he died in a plane crash over North Africa in his B-17 a month after I was born, so he never saw me. Trying to reconstruct a ghost was challenging and frustrating. My mother remarried and had four more children. My stepfather was anything but encouraging about my quest for my roots, as everyone had lied to me about who this man was that I found written about in a baby book with my name on it. I started developing empathy for adopted children, and started dealing with the alcoholism in several generations of my family.

I obviously felt the need to learn through my own laboratory so I married an alcoholic and tried "to get it right" through my own experience. The marriage lasted twenty years and produced two fabulous children that are now servant leaders in their own rights. I really started to understand the disease of codependency and the crazy behavior displayed by persons who were married to folks who had addictions. The codependents can be seen as quite crazy by their behavior, and the addicts can appear quite charming and indignant. About this time, I started developing empathy for divorcing parties and the effect that divorce had on children, again learning in my own laboratory. After our divorce, I started practicing law, and utilizing the law degree I had received after attending law school at night while serving fifteen years in the administration at Rice University, raising two children, ages four and six, and dealing with an impaired spouse. While at Rice I taught, but mostly was a therapist and the administrator in charge of all student personnel projects such as yearbook, newspaper, radio station, etc. I was involved in team building with a wonderful group of really talented young student leaders. Many of the students I worked with at Rice are presently leading Houston and Harris County (the mayor, county judge and commissioner, and more). I could not be more proud of having watched them grow from college kids to the servant leaders they are today. It is an honor to know these people and call them my friends. I have served as a mentor for many years in all my professions, and received the "Mentor Recognition Award" at Rice before I departed to start helping folks using my law degree. I never had dreams of law making me wealthy. I truly went into the field with the intention of helping others.

One of my life long convictions is that real sin is being given a gift by God that you do not use to help others. I firmly believe that nothing you learn is useless. As I tried to figure out how this latest lesson I learned fits into what I am supposed to learn in this life, and how I can turn it to be something I can use to help others, I took the experience of realizing my own codependency to study and became licensed as a Chemical Dependence Specialist, and then later an Advanced Addiction Counselor.

I am also a Licensed Marriage and Family Therapist. All this assisted me mightily as I started my next career as a family law attorney.

In the mean time, I was selected for *Leadership Houston*. It was a wonderfully expanding experience that exposed me to the inner workings of Houston and those who really made the decisions around the important sectors of our community. The added benefit was to make friends with people from other parts of our community that I would never have met otherwise. We concentrated on team building a class project in *Leadership Houston*. This required active listening and a greater understanding of the marvelous diversity that Houston is. Once you develop a relationship with and have empathy for someone from a religion, race, belief system or anything else unlike yours, the preconceived notions you harbored about that group begin to melt away. It is not unlike loosening a corset and being able to breathe free from constraining, stuck in concrete feelings and beliefs. What a joy! This kind of training continued in my life by having been selected to be in classes of *Leadership America* and *American Leadership Forum*. I guess I am drawn to organizations with "Leadership" in their title! The corset was loosened even more in these two organizations and the tapestry of my life became richer and more diverse.

I practiced law and continued raising my children but was given the greatest gift of another chance at love. I fell in love with and married an ex-pro-football player who had owned numerous businesses. He has since returned to law school and is now a practicing attorney and mediator. He is the essence of a servant leader, mentoring and teaching new attorneys, and representing children in court. I led by example and showed my children how a great relationship should work. This time my own laboratory has been joyfully successful as we have been on a continuing honeymoon for the last twenty-two years.

After practicing law for ten years and witnessing firsthand the practice of judges taking campaign money from lawyers that practiced in front of them, and feeling numerous times as though those that had given to the judges were perhaps in a better position than those who had not given, I decided to run for judge. I vowed never to take money from lawyers that practice family law because I never wanted there to be a question about the rulings I made. It felt like the difference between knowing the right thing and then doing the right thing. Let me explain that my stance on this issue was difficult, as no one really cares about the judicial races unless they practice in that court, and I was the only one to have this ethic. When I retire in the end of 2014, after twenty years on the bench, I can proudly say I have maintained that stance and have won five elections without taking one dime from a lawyer who practices in my court.

Once I was elected in 1994, I started trying to imagine how I could gather all I had learned to benefit the public I was serving. The collaborative skills and people I had learned from in the various leadership groups came in really handy when I combined them with my knowledge of the addictions, the law, counseling practices and team building. We started the first and only *Family Intervention Court* in Harris County in my court, which is a treatment court to assist parents with alcohol and drug problems who have had their children removed from their custody. We have combined the treatment providers, Children Protective Services, County attorneys, the court, private practice lawyers, counselors, *Houston Works*, and many others to provide fabulous wrap around services for these victims. Additionally, in the past three years we have added a component that looks at the particular needs of the children of these relationships and getting them the special services they will need. We are concentrating on attachment disorders and the effects of alcohol and drug exposure during fetal development. It is now becoming a state and national model, and we are all very proud of the work we are doing to help those affected by the family cycle of addiction. My other goal is to turn the participants from takers into givers. Unfortunately, our society has produced several generations of folks who believe that their job is to live on state and federal handouts, so education, marriage and jobs, are not part of their life plans. Frequently, this profile also intersects with our drug court population. We work to make sure they have the minimum: a GED, a job and stable housing so they can then offer their children examples of how to live a clean and sober life, and how to give back to the community. It is a beautiful thing to watch self esteem develop before your eyes. I guess this is being a grandparent servant leader.

Looking back, I would not do anything differently. My son is a Major in the Army as an Emergency Room physician. He and his wife (a pediatrician and an internist) have two children. My daughter is a marriage and family therapist married to a veterinarian surgeon and they have two children. Both are heavily involved in their churches and community, and are blessings to this world. I would never have had them had

I not made the original choice to marry their father. I also would have never been an attorney and therefore a judge had I not married my first husband, but I would never have been happy like I have been without the love of my life. All I have accomplished in the court for the families has been with his help and guidance. For however long I have, I hope I can continue to make a difference in the lives of those with whom I come in contact. It has been a joyous and fulfilling ride and I am grateful. I have lived a lot, both for me and for my father, who didn't have the chance.

THE
Practice
OF
Servant
LEADERSHIP

LAURENCE J. "LARRY" PAYNE

THE CONTEXT FOR SERVANT LEADERSHIP & HOW IT WORKS

A SERVANT LEADER IS A SERVANT FIRST, A LEADER LAST

A servant leader takes care of others first. This means administering to others, customer service, teambuilding and teaching. Though you might think a servant leader would be the more unfocused member of the team, they are in fact the glue that bonds people together to create success.

A servant leader is a person of vision. There is always tension between vision and reality. Max De Pree, CEO of Herman Miller Inc., defines reality as the first responsibility of a servant leader, but equally important is holding people to the vision. Great leaders hold people firmly in the tension that exists between vision and reality.

Perhaps this model will help—the *Triangle of Vision*. Take a rubber band: stretch it between your thumb and forefinger with one hand, and with the other hand pull down on the bottom until the rubber band takes the shape of an upside down triangle. This physically represents the relationship between vision and reality. Your life and your business are always changing, so your reality is, too. Reality pulls down, away from the top rung, which is your vision. Reality is always in flux, moving towards or away from the top portion of your rubber band, the vision.

The servant leader thrives in this dynamic tension between reality and vision; he or she will keep this triangle structurally sound, never allowing reality to ascend too quickly to the vision, never allowing vision to move out of sight and therefore become unobtainable. Servant leaders are the pace cars on the track—they guide the team, keep everyone in alignment and remain steady in the reality of the present moment.

A SERVANT LEADER IS WHOLE

To keep others in alignment, a leader must be whole. There are three parts to each of us that must be in alignment for us to be whole: the head, the heart and the gut. How do you ensure that each of these key aspects of your life is fully functional?

- **The Head:** The head encompasses your thinking, your message, the ways you understand and communicate. Ask yourself, "What do I think and believe?" The answer should not be what people and policies want you to think and believe, but what your head tells you independently of those outside factors.

- **The Heart:** The heart represents your feelings, the affective part of your vision, the soul. Your mission is a heart element. When you align your heart, you reflect on what you feel and how you feel about what you think. This is soul-searching, identifying the mores and values you hold, or would like to hold.
- **The Gut:** The gut is what you actually do—your actions, behaviors and the results they get. This part of your being requires you to let go of negatives in order to take on positives. There is not room for both to function proactively.

If any of these areas is out of alignment, not functioning properly, you're like a wheel that cannot roll—you're missing a necessary piece of yourself. To align these parts of your being and to attune yourself as a servant leader, you need to value taking time to think, to reflect and to meditate. Time to be by yourself to consider head, heart and gut, uninfluenced, is key to the building of wholeness—and you cannot begin to be selfless without making the self whole first.

A servant leader is cognizant of other's thoughts and feelings. You engage team members and those you are leading, let them know they are valued and offer rewards and incentives to help encourage proactive behavior and leadership potential. Servant leadership is all about changing attitudes through these actions and behaviors, on a daily basis. You can think and feel all day long, but if you do not act, change is never implemented, skills are left in the classroom, deals are left on the table and faith is left where it was first preached or developed. Leadership lives, enables and inspires through actions.

ROBERT GREENLEAF'S TEN PRINCIPLES OF SERVANT LEADERSHIP

- **Listening:** Traditionally, leaders have been valued for their communication and decision-making skills. Servant leaders must reinforce these important skills by making a deep commitment to listening intently to others. Servant leaders seek to identify and clarify the will of a group. They seek to listen receptively to what is being said (and not said). Listening also encompasses getting in touch with one's inner voice, and seeking to understand what one's body, spirit and mind are communicating.

  Listening is the key characteristic for servant leadership. A servant leader must first and always be an active listener. This is necessary in order to give feedback, to internalize others. Being an effective listener is an attitude toward people as much as it is an action. Listeners observe the topic and the feedback given by others; they ask questions in order to listen more effectively, to learn about themselves as well as others. Servant leaders are valued for their communication skills and their decision-making skills—which begin and end with listening to those they are building a relationship with.

- **Empathy:** Servant leaders strive to understand and empathize with others. People need to be accepted and recognized for their special and unique spirit. One must assume the good intentions of coworkers and not reject them as people, even when forced to reject their behavior or performance.

  Without empathy toward others a leader cannot connect and build relationships, communities, businesses and schools, or take on medical endeavors of lasting proportions. A servant leader recognizes and accepts other's viewpoints as she would want her own to be received. If you're in the service industry it is putting yourself on the other side of a table and empathizing with guests as to the type of dining experience you would like to receive; if it is in the medical field you put yourself as the patient and care as you would want to be cared for; in business it's creating the respect across a table and diplomatically solving a problem in a way that profits and maintains a mission and creates a greater good for all parties involved; in education empathy comes in how we educate our future's children—we ask how we would like our own children educated and we then foster that experience within the classrooms.

- **Healing (and Overcoming Fear):** Learning to heal is a powerful force for transformation and integration. One of the great strengths of servant leadership is the potential for healing one's self and others. In *The Servant as Leader* Greenleaf writes, "There is something subtle communicated to one who is being served and led if, implicit in the compact between the servant leader and led is the understanding that the search for wholeness is something that they have."

  As integral as healing is, it is not possible to heal without first overcoming the fear that fuels it. You cannot begin to lead others if you have not first eliminated the fear that propels you, in turn allowing the healing process to begin. To lead a person by helping them overcome their fears is one of the greatest, most influential strengths a servant leader can possess and impose on those they lead.

- **Awareness:** Awareness is not a giver of solace—it's just the opposite. It disturbs. They [servant leaders] are not seekers of solace. They have their own inner security. General awareness, and especially self-awareness, strengthens the servant leader. Making a commitment to foster awareness can be scary—one never knows what one may discover!

  Confidence is awareness, as this creates the security necessary to lead others.

- **Persuasion:** Servant leaders rely on persuasion, rather than positional authority in making decisions. Servant leaders seek to convince others, rather than coerce compliance. This particular element offers one of the clearest distinctions between the traditional authoritarian model and that of servant leadership. The servant leader is effective at building consensus within groups.

  As a servant leader you want your team to buy into your purpose, your mission, your goal. Rather than forcing people to work toward your goal, structuring parameters for compliance, whole-heartedly believing in a purpose and collectively reaching an end-goal creates much sweeter success.

- **Conceptualization:** Servant leaders seek to nurture their abilities to "dream great dreams." The ability to look at a problem (or an organization) from a conceptualizing perspective means that one must think beyond day-to-day realities. Servant leaders must seek a delicate balance between conceptualization and day-to-day focus.

    Servant leaders have the ability to see past today and into tomorrow. They believe that today is about tomorrow, and the tomorrow after tomorrow. They take hold of a community, a problem, an organization or a task and foster the growth and development needed to achieve success.

- **Foresight:** Foresight is a characteristic that enables servant leaders to understand lessons from the past, the realities of the present, and the likely consequence of a decision in the future. It is deeply rooted in the intuitive mind.

    This servant leadership characteristic enables you to process fundamental lessons from previous circumstances, incorporate them into the present realities and execute a decisive future for your community or group. This characteristic is deeply rooted in the intuitive mind of leaders as they rely on not only what they think, but heavily on how they feel in their gut. This ties back into aligning the head/the heart/ the gut—the thinking/ feeling/acting.

- **Stewardship:** In the servant leadership vision, CEOs, staff, directors, and trustees all play significant roles in holding their institutions in trust for the great good of society.

    You cannot create lasting results without holding yourself, your team and your company accountable to a mission or policy that serves the greater good. Your time, talent, treasure and touch should all be utilized toward this end.

- **Commitment to the Growth of People:** Servant leaders believe that people have an intrinsic value beyond their tangible contributions as workers. As such, servant leaders are deeply committed to a personal, professional and spiritual growth of each and every individual within the organization.

This commitment is foremost to the self. You must first make the commitment of servant leadership to yourself before you can commit to others. This is also a commitment to listening to others, a commitment to purpose and a commitment to self-development through learning, teaching and healing.

- **Building Community:** Servant leaders are aware that the shift from local communities to large institutions as the primary shaper of human lives has changed our perceptions and has caused a feeling of loss. Servant leaders seek to identify a means for building community among those who work within a given institution.

  Servant leadership roles can shift rather quickly and unexpectedly, and leaders are ever aware that their impact from local communities and institutions to larger ones means they are primary shapers of other's lives. The loss of a servant leader is monumental, changing perceptions and leaving a wake for fellow servant leaders to take charge. These next-generation servant leaders identify the means for others to continue community building after the original leader moves on to serve in a broader way.

BUYING INTO THE PURPOSE

If you've ever wondered why strong leaders have such devout followers, it is because they have been able to sell their purpose well. Companies get employees to buy into their mission by daily adhering to the actions and behaviors (gut) that reflection and research (heart and head) have shown to be beneficial. We cannot hear it often enough: Consistency is the key to change—to changing bad habits into good habits, to changing our mission or purpose, study habits or any regular behavior.

RELATIONSHIP BUILDING 101

Leaders achieve buy-in to their purpose by handling relationships with a fundamental approach. This one idea is a springboard for virtually everything servant leader related, life related and business related. Every deal begins with a connection. A relationship develops, and then one visionary or another sees potential and acts.

What is the approach that makes it work? Act with mutual respect and trust. That's it. This one concept is the key to building lasting relationships in any of these sectors. With the trust and respect of your team, you will almost always get to the truth of any matter. If you build a foundation upon these two ideas it cements the entire structure of your endeavor. Every one of the men and women in this book has practiced this concept. This approach, coupled with their dedication to their respective causes, makes their stories as inspirational as they are. True servant leaders do not need to be reminded that each person they lead is entitled to this trust and respect, or that every human being deserves it.

Once the foundation of mutual respect and trust has been established, a servant leader acts with sincerity and selflessness. The lasting relationships created this way forge a bond that builds teams. Without these strong bonds, the men and women who lead by their service to the community would not have seen their purposes, missions and successes come to fruition.

THE HEXAGONAL TRUTH

A servant leader recognizes the hexagonal truth, that there are five versions to every story: his, hers, theirs, the devil's and the truth. The leader also recognizes that myth, rumor, opinion, fact and truth can all pass for the same thing today. Recognizing this subjectivity, being able to see through perspective-oriented detail and recognize the realities of a given situation, a servant leader gains the insight that is needed to build relationships. This objectivity is an essential point-of-view for managing any situation and using energy to work toward the real purpose of the team.

SERVANT LEADERSHIP AS A MANAGEMENT TECHNIQUE

Servant leadership helps grow your company and develops your employees and their potential. You may wonder if the skills necessary for servant leadership, or for teaching servant leadership as a management technique, are innate to only some people, or if they can be learned. The answer to these questions is both yes and no. In some instances, a leader is born; in others, created or molded.

Your lowest-selling employee can become your top gross-generating employee; your team member with the worst attitude and customer service skills can become your most personable team member; and your most hedonistic congregant can become a faith leader in his own right someday. If you were not born with the traits of a leader, you can be taught the skill set a leader possesses—you need only to examine your heart, align your inward thoughts and beliefs with your outward actions and behaviors, set the standard and lead by example. Others will follow, because they recognize the importance of what you are doing, or because they fear being left off the bandwagon. And thus, servant leadership is fostered to spread throughout your organization and eventually through the community you touch.

LEARNING AND LEADING BY EXAMPLE

The lessons taken from the essays collected in this book can be used as practical examples of how to change your mindset to that of a servant leader. They can be applied to any position held in any field or sector. The most important thing to remember is that no matter what business you are in, you are in the people business first. If you exemplify servant leadership in your treatment of employees, they in turn will do the same for your customers, guests, associates, clients, congregants, patients or anyone your enterprise touches. This leadership rule will always lend the results sought—success in your endeavor. For some leaders, success is return business from loyal patrons, and for others it is the satisfaction of watching a project unfold and manifest its greatest potential.

Check List for Leaders

- **Do** your personal, professional and public lives need to be aligned? In Harper Lee's *To Kill a Mockingbird*, Atticus Finch was known by his character; he was the same person in public that he was in private. This integrity makes for a respected, powerful servant leader. Can you say the same about yourself? If not, what do you need to change?
- **Do** your employees identify with the brand promise, the end product of the project? Do they learn it, live it and then lead with it?
- **Do** you regularly identify where your mission statement is out of alignment? Where your employees are not aligning with that mission? You can do this with focus groups and workshops.
- **Do** you value your team members for what they bring to the company culture, both strengths and opportunities for growth?

LOVE THE ONE YOU'RE WITH

The formula for any successful bottom line is ***people + profits = success.*** You cannot have a profitable equation without first having the people to ensure that success will take shape. The servant leadership business practice is one in which the people involved come first. You can think of it like this: *You must love the one you're with, and with that one you will grow.* This means real commitment to the people you're involved with, the people who are your team members, working for and with you. You all have the same end-goal in mind—success.

To successfully practice servant leadership as a management technique, you'll need to assess and reassess regularly. Ask yourself if you are doing the following:

- *Employee/team member growth—is it your number one concern, more so than whatever you are producing, building or selling.* If you are growing and developing your people they will want to share that knowledge base with others, to teach that knowledge to others. It is a great feeling to share the breadth of your knowledge and skills to help a person develop to his or her fullest potential. The fulfillment felt on every level when you take this approach fosters the mission of your business.
- *The quality of the interactions with people—team members as*

well as those being served—is a priority. Make time for the people in your community or on your team—your employees, customers and family—they in turn will make time for you. You cannot expect to be their first priority if you have not shown interest or taken value in those you lead and serve. This is a two-way street.

- *You practice the ethical treatment of employees.* Forget the issue of diversity; we have moved past it. We are all human beings first and foremost, and should be treated fairly and justly based on that one criterion alone. If you remember this one piece of information, live this one value, servant leadership is at your fingertips.
- *You are outer-centered.* In order for leadership as a servant to work for you and your purpose, you must remember, "It's about my people, not me." Jim Collins notes that a servant leader is a level five person. He says, "They channel their egos away from themselves and into the larger goal of building [greatness]...their ambition is on the institution, not themselves." Nothing lasting, progressive and constructive ever happens if we are only looking out for ourselves.

SIX REASONS WHY SERVANT LEADERSHIP WORKS AS A MANAGEMENT TECHNIQUE

1. *Servant leadership fosters an atmosphere of teamwork.* This is the *Us* thinking vs. the *I* thinking. Productivity and creativity increase when competition is removed from the equation.

2. *Servant leadership increases your potential for success.* Remember, singly you are limited by your talents and abilities alone, whereas with the combined talents, abilities and creativity of a team you can break the ceiling for success's limit.

3. *Servant leadership adds value to the members of your team.* If you fail to give your team a sense of value, they fail to see the value in their leader, their work and their commitment to the purpose and mission statement of the company. Your team needs to know they are valued for more than just getting the job done.

4. *Servant leadership fosters an atmosphere of trust.* When employees feel cared for and trusted, there is no room for backbiting and distrust.

Trust thrives where trust is planted. When employees feel that they are trusted to perform, they then trust in their leaders. This is guidance. A sheep trusts that his shepherd will lead him to pasture based on past experiences with the shepherd; a shepherd in turn trusts that the sheep will follow him to pasture based on his past experience with the sheep. It's all a matter of leading by example and following through.

5. *Servant leadership reaps what it sows.* If you are self-serving, no one trusts your motives, and you then encourage self-serving behaviors in your team. However, if you encourage service to others first, your team will in turn serve selflessly, creating an atmosphere that will thrive on success. Servant leadership is properly cultivating relationships. You are foremost in the people business, no matter what your business is— remember that. You lead—not food, not money, not products, but people—to success. You give service and respect first, and other benefits will follow, profits will follow, repeat business will follow and people will follow, and then be inspired.

6. *Servant leadership makes its leaders their own CEOs.* In essence, this forces you to lead and manage as you would wish to be led and managed. You ask how a person would like to be served, and serve them in such a way. You ask a person how best you can manage them, and by managing them you are helping them to grow, develop and overcome obstacles and barriers that hinder their performance. You help them to reach their God-given potential—and then you follow through with consistency. By making each of your team members his or her own CEO, you are enabling them to gather a breadth of knowledge and insight that you would otherwise never be able to tap.

GO FORTH AND SERVE

The examples of the men and women in this book serve as testament to the power of servant leadership to enrich the lives of all involved and create greater opportunities for success. Robert Greenleaf's paradigm is life changing. There is no limit to the ways the practice of servant leadership can be employed. Don't worry if it seems that your own goals are taking a backseat to the group. That means you're doing it right. Servant leadership is group-goal-oriented first; personal goals come to fruition through the success of the group.

The late Stephen Covey believed in principle-centered leadership—to build character and trust is to build greatness. Put the focus on "I" behind you, and you'll see how great you, your organization and all of us, can be together. Build a strong foundation on integrity, fairness, kindness, efficiency, effectiveness, communication and vision. Clarify what you mean by greatness, make your behavior congruent with that belief, and align your actions with your goals. You will lead your organization to more meaningful success than you can imagine, and the process will be as enriching as reaching the goal.

THE HOUSTON FACTOR

Culture that built city can be a key to success

By Ed Wulfe

Albert Einstein wrote that "Not everything that counts can be counted," and I think that message really applies to Houston. For many months, we have heard nothing but negative statistics, data and projections on the state of our economy.

But what counts the most for us, that no one is talking about, is something I'm calling the Houston Factor. You can't quantify it. There's no way to explain it in numbers or percentages. But it is special and it is our culture.

Look at what happened after the Allen brothers arrived here and saw a swampy bayou and envisioned a great city; or when Jesse Jones managed to save all the Houston banks during the Great Depression. We had leaders who got the Port of Houston built 50 miles from the Gulf. One of the greatest medical centers in the world was conceived and built attracting the best in medicine. Our resiliency got us back in record time after the battering from Hurricane Ike.

How does this kind of thing happen in Houston year after year, decade after decade? How do we build on it?

To be successful in business or in any undertaking, you must be an optimist with a can-do attitude. We're a city optimists in a welcoming and entrepreneurial environment with the passion and energy to make things happen. A can-do mentality is our heritage. That's the Houston Factor—and it's something that other cities just don't have. The Houston Factor has made the difference, and it will again.

We've been through tough economical times before. I remember the downturn in the '70s; the foreclosed properties and the saving and loan busts of the '80s, and we had some rough bumps in the '90s. Cycles come and go.

But, as in the past, Houston is blessed by the fact that we're not feeling the impact to the extent that other cities are.

Build your skills. Volunteer and help others. Be a team player. Be both responsive and responsible. That's the Houston Factor.

In fact, we're beginning to see light at the end of the tunnel so we need to be persistent, figure out how to adapt and change for what's next, and stay upbeat and positive. Positive energy and passion go a long way—the Houston factor.

So, what's your mindset? Are you working on expanding your network? We live in a friendly and open city.

Now more than ever, you should be reaching out and growing your relationships and contacts in your field and in our civic and cultural communities.

Houstonians know how to work harder and understand you must be aggressive and make things happen. They know they need to add value. That's the Houston Factor. They understand the need to get out there and concentrate on what you're doing and on your business, whether you are an employee or employer.

Houstonians believe in themselves, their business, and their city. They are leaders and innovators who are eager to learn more and grown as a person. Now is when you must become better informed and better equipped. Build your skills. Volunteer and help others. Be a team player. Be both responsive and responsible. That's the Houston Factor. Besides your business and job, are you marketing yourself? Most people don't look at themselves as a brand. And they don't consider how to market that brand. We all should be doing that and, at the same time, marketing the Houston Factor.

Are you envisioning what's next? Visioning is a big part of the Houston Factor. Where do you want to be when this ends? Because it will end and we'll be back in new ways for exciting times. Houstonians are always ready to seize the moment. We have the Houston Factor on our side. Are you capitalizing on it?

Ed Wulfe is Founder and President of Wulfe &Co., a Houston based commercial real estate development, brokerage and property management firm. Wulfe is a civic and community activist and has served many organizations in a leadership role.

As appeared in the Houston Chronicle *Monday, May 4, 2009.*

BIBLIOGRAPHY

Buber, Martin. *Teaching and Deed.* Palgrave Macmillan. Ed. 1. 2002.

Collins, Jim. *Good to Great.* Harper Business. 2001.

Covey, Stephen. *The 8th Habit: From Effectiveness to Greatness.* Simon and Schuster. 2013.

De Pree, Max. *Leadership is an Art.* Random House. 2011.

Good, David. "5 Reasons Why Servant Leadership Works." *Technorati Guru.* 28 June 2011. Web. 14 Nov. 2013.

Greenleaf, Robert K. *The Servant as Leader.* Indianapolis, IN: Robert K. Greenleaf Center, 1991. Print.

Greenleaf, Robert. "The Principles of Servant Leadership." *Butler University.* Web. 14 Nov. 2013.

Haden, Jeff. "5 Underrated Traits of Great Leaders." *Inc.com.* Inc., 6 Sept. 2012. Web. 14 Nov. 2013.

Haden, Jeff. "Do You Pass This Key Leadership Test?" *Inc.com.* Inc., 4 Sept. 2012. Web. 14 Nov. 2013.

Haden, Jeff. "Best Way to Make Employees Better at Their Jobs." *Inc.com.* Inc., 23 July 2012. Web. 14 Nov. 2013.

Haden, Jeff. "10 (More) Beliefs of Remarkably Successful People." *Inc.com.* Inc., 2012. Web. 14 Nov. 2013.

Holy Bible, KJV. Zondervan. 2011.

James, Geoffrey. "World's Simplest Management Secret." *Inc.com.* Inc., 24 Oct. 2012. Web. 14 Nov. 2013.

Knudsen, E., Heckman, J., Cameron, J., & Shonkoff, J. (2006). *Proceedings of the National Academy of Sciences, 103, 10155-10162.* Defending Childhood: Keeping the Promise of Early Education. Teachers College Press. New York. 2012.

Jaworski, Joseph. *Synchronicity: The Inner Path of Leadership.* California: Berrett-Koehler. 2011. 19-20.

L., Michael. Weblog comment. "What Management Techniques Demonstrate Servant Leadership?" *LinkedIn.com.* LinkedIn, Jan. 2013. Web. 14 Nov. 2013. (zig zigler comment)

Lee, Harper. *To Kill A Mockingbird.* J. B. Lippincott & Co. 1960.

Robinson, Charles. "Essay on Servant Leadership." *Articlesbase.com.* Articlesbase, 9 Jan. 2010. Web. 14 Nov. 2013.

Wiesel, Elie. *The Gates of the Forest.* Schocken Books Inc. 1995.

Wulfe, Ed. "Make Most of the Houston Factor: Culture That Built City Can Be a Key to Success." *Houston Chronicle* [Houston] 4 May 2009: n. page. Print.